Planning & Remodeling
Kitchens

By the Editors of Sunset Books and Sunset Magazine

Lane Publishing Co.• Menlo Park, California

Edited by Maureen Williams Zimmerman

Design: Joe di Chiarro
Artwork: Joe Seney

Cover: Overhead rack for pots and pans is just
one of many functional, attractive features of
this remodeled kitchen (see page 29).
Photographed by Darrow M. Watt.

Editor, Sunset Books: David E. Clark

Seventh printing April 1982

Contents

Planning: Where all good kitchens begin

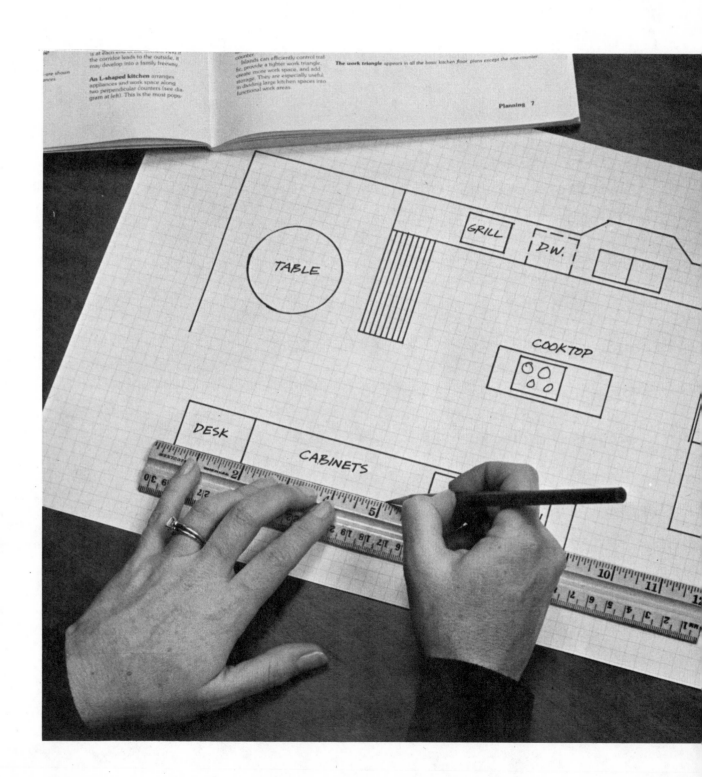

Around the turn of the century, it was fashionable to ignore the kitchen's existence—cooking was done in the nether regions of the house, often by servants.

Fashions change. Now, attention is focused on the kitchen—we acknowledge it as the busy center of household activity. The well-designed kitchen of today should not only be pleasing to the eye but should reflect the individual needs, work habits, and entertaining styles of members of the household.

You can plan an efficient kitchen that will meet your needs and your wants, as well as your budget. To help you, this chapter presents suggestions for kitchen planning; concrete information on dimensions, building materials, and appliances; and guidelines for working with designers and contractors, as well as for doing the work yourself. You can include and adapt the ideas that are best for you.

Where to begin?

The best-laid plans may shift and change in the shuffle of building, but that doesn't make planning any less important.

Thoroughly evaluating the needs of both family and cook and accurately planning all features should produce a workable, efficient kitchen plan.

Think about the various family activities that depend on a functional kitchen. Does your family gather for regular meals three times a day, or do the activities of family members require something resembling an all-day smorgasbord? Do you want to eliminate family traffic in kitchen work areas during meal preparation?

How frequently do you entertain? Is most entertaining formal or informal? Does more than one member of the family actively participate in the cooking?

A self-appraisal by the cook is the next step. Is cooking a joy or a necessary evil? Is a neat-as-a-pin kitchen essential to your well-being, or do open shelves and hanging utensils create a working environment that you find pleasant?

Look at your present kitchen. . . . What do you like about its efficiency and appearance? What do you dislike?

Which appliances with their new features will be indispensable to your new kitchen? On pages 13–16 you'll find information that will help you decide which appliances you need and which you can do without.

Have you always wished for a baking center or a kitchen office or an indoor barbecue? Now is the time to plan for it. These and other special centers are discussed on pages 9–11.

As you consider these questions, some possible kitchen floor plans will probably be materializing. The actual floor plan begins with decisions on the basic kitchen layout to be used, the position of the work triangle (the triangle formed by the placement of the sink, refrigerator, and range; see pages 7–8), and the specialized work centers to be incorporated.

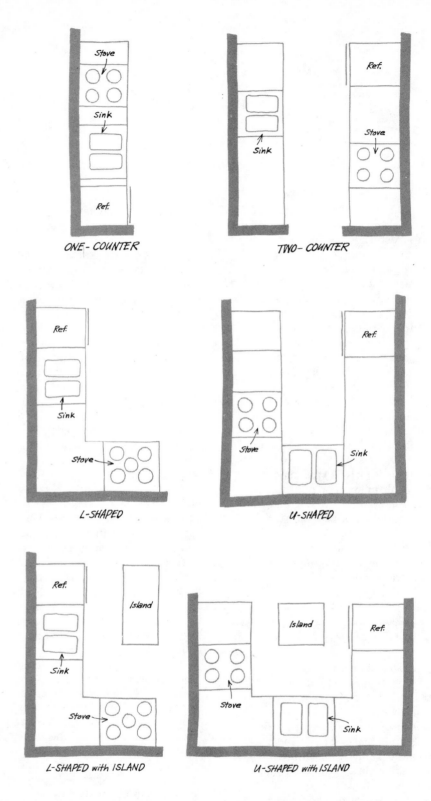

ONE-COUNTER

TWO-COUNTER

L-SHAPED

U-SHAPED

L-SHAPED with ISLAND

U-SHAPED with ISLAND

Six basic floor plans—*including two variations of the island plan—are shown above. Each plan illustrates possible placement of three main appliances.*

Here are basic kitchen floor plans

Five basic layouts stand out in kitchen design today. Defined according to the shape in which counters are arranged (regardless of whether a counter is built against a wall or is freestanding), they are 1) a one-counter or strip kitchen; 2) a two-counter, corridor, or pullman kitchen; 3) an L-shaped kitchen; 4) a U-shaped kitchen; 5) a kitchen with an island.

Each of these kitchen floor plans presents both advantages and disadvantages, and all have numerous variations—the U-shaped kitchen, for example, can become round or octagonal.

A one-counter or strip kitchen, commonly used in such small-space situations as apartments or vacation cabins, positions all appliances and work areas in one row. A single-counter plan is most efficient when the sink is centrally located and the total length is under 22 feet.

The main disadvantage is that distances between work areas tend to be long, since a one-counter kitchen doesn't allow a work triangle.

A two-counter, corridor, or pullman kitchen divides appliances and work areas between two parallel counters. (Parallel counters should be separated by at least 4 feet of clear space; 5 feet if two or more people will be working at the same time.) This arrangement creates a work triangle, usually provides ample counter space, and is generally a very economical type of kitchen to build.

Its main disadvantage is that the corridor between the two counters encourages foot traffic if a doorway is at each end of the kitchen. And if the corridor leads to the outside, it may develop into a family freeway.

An L-shaped kitchen arranges appliances and work space along two perpendicular counters (see diagram at left). This is the most popular kitchen plan because it adapts to a wide variety of arrangements.

Frequently one "leg" of the L doubles as a room divider. This plan frees floor space for other uses and directs traffic away from the cook's work area.

Placing the sink and appliances can be a challenge, though. If the sink, refrigerator, and cooktop are too far apart, the work triangle will be exhausting.

The U-shaped kitchen requires lots of space but is considered by many experts to be the most efficient floor plan because of its compact work triangle and the easy separation of the work area from family traffic patterns.

This floor plan divides appliances and work areas among three connected counters arranged in a U. Any or all parts of the U may extend into the room without wall support. Generally, the sink is placed at the base of the U, the range or cooktop and the refrigerator on the facing legs. The result is a tight work triangle that eliminates wasted effort. Counter space is continuous, and ample storage is made available.

Problems arise if the kitchen is too small (less than 6 feet between base cabinets). Minor disadvantages are the extensive countertops—possibly more than you'll have use for—and the need for special cabinets to utilize the corners.

Island kitchens have helped expand these basic floor plans in recent years. All layouts except the pullman kitchen can benefit from the addition of an island.

Freestanding and usually centrally located, an island can be mobile, adding extra work space wherever needed. If it isn't mobile, it may contain a sink or cooktop. An island can also provide an eating counter.

Islands can efficiently control traffic, provide a tighter work triangle, create more work space, and add storage. They are especially useful in dividing large kitchen spaces into functional work areas.

The work triangle: easy geometry for kitchen planners

After you determine the shape your new kitchen will take, consider appliance placement next. The three main work centers—sink, refrigerator, and range or cooktop—should form a triangle whose three sides total no less than 12 feet and no more than 22 feet. This is called the work triangle.

The easiest way to experiment with the work triangle arrangement

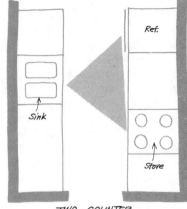

TWO-COUNTER

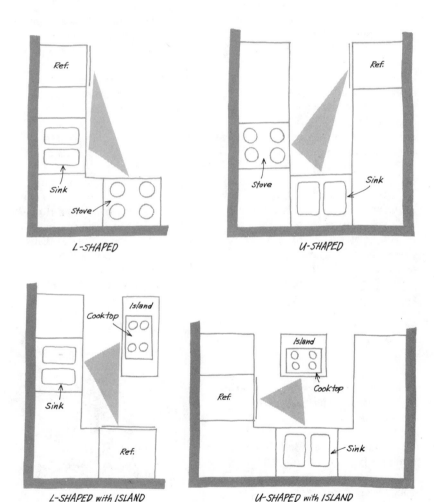

L-SHAPED

U-SHAPED

L-SHAPED with ISLAND

U-SHAPED with ISLAND

The work triangle appears in all the basic kitchen floor plans except the one-counter.

is to make a simple scale model of your kitchen design. Draw an outline of your kitchen on ¼-inch graph paper, measuring ¼ inch—one square of the grid—for each foot of actual size. Then cut out shapes to represent the appliances (size ranges for each appliance are given on pages 13–16), still using ¼ inch to represent each foot. Move the cutouts around on the graph paper until the work triangle suits you. Then add the cabinets and any special work centers to scale.

The distance between refrigerator and sink should be 4 to 7 feet; between sink and range, 4 to 6 feet; range and refrigerator, 4 to 9 feet. If oven and cooktop are separate units, the oven may be located outside the triangle.

A work triangle in this size range allows for enough counter and storage space so work isn't cramped, yet arranges appliances and their related centers (see below) so the cook won't cover great distances during meal preparation.

Because more trips are made between sink and range than between any other two work centers, this leg of the triangle is often the shortest.

As you plan, try to locate the triangle out of the way of foot traffic. Plan adequate aisles between activity centers to allow for easy movement. Between opposite work counters, allow at least 48 inches; if two or more people are likely to be sharing the kitchen, allow 54 to 64 inches.

Kitchen centers divide the chores

The military strategy of divide and conquer is a good one for the kitchen planner. With space divided into specialized work areas, the related tasks become easier to perform, and the final outcome is an efficient, functional kitchen—a sure victory for the designer and the cook.

Some centers are basic

Since each kitchen task requires a particular working surface and/or appliance, as well as specialized tools and necessary ingredients, it makes sense to organize centers by locating the needed equipment with the appliances in an adequate work area.

Four centers are basic to most kitchens: a sink or cleanup center, a refrigerator center, a preparation or mix center, and a cooking center. Other more specialized areas—a baking or serving center, for example—can increase kitchen efficiency.

Since the sink area is used most frequently, it is often the first planned.

The sink center handles food washing and trimming, dish clean-up, and garbage disposal. Appliances include a sink, a mechanical garbage disposer, a dishwasher, and sometimes a trash compactor placed nearby.

Counters are needed on both sides of the sink: one 3 feet wide on one side for stacking dirty dishes and one 2½ feet wide on the other side for draining dishes. A dishwasher is commonly placed to the left of the sink; a left-handed person, though, may prefer to have it on the right.

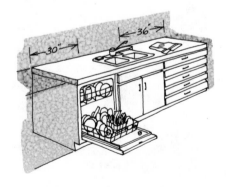

Provide storage for soap and other cleaning materials and towels near the sink. Locate dish and flatware storage close to the dishwasher for easy unloading.

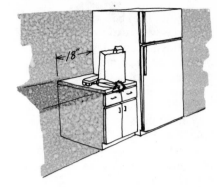

The refrigerator center handles the storage of perishable foods. A refrigerator/freezer combination or a separate freezer unit allows longer storage of many foods. An infrequently used freezer, though, may best be located in an adjacent utility room or in the garage, freeing valuable kitchen space.

A counter approximately 1½ feet wide located on the door latch side of the refrigerator serves as a landing pad for groceries on their way to and from refrigeration.

Ideally, the refrigerator center should be near both the preparation center and the doorway through which you'll be bringing groceries.

Because the refrigerator works by dissipating heat, and the range creates heat, it is inefficient to put the refrigerator next to the range. When the two are in close contact, heat from the range interferes somewhat with the refrigerator's cooling system.

The preparation center is the place for mixing and preparing foods prior to cooking or serving them. A 3 to 3½-foot counter is recommended, with a surface for cutting and chopping either built in or readily available. An electrical outlet for a food processor, mixer, and other small appliances used in food preparation is handy. Sometimes a lower-than-usual counter is used here.

Ample storage for dry ingredients, baking pans, casseroles, and utensils needed for measuring and mixing will be helpful. Good knife storage can be incorporated. The best place for this center is near the refrigerator and/or the sink.

In this center, storage presents a challenge. Small appliances used in food preparation—such as a mixer, blender, and can opener—need carefully planned storage, for if they aren't kept handy, you may not use them. Where counter space is limited, an appliance compartment may be the answer.

The cooking center contains either a cooktop with separate oven or a range. (A separate oven may be located anywhere in the kitchen, but generally is near the cooktop.)

Place a counter at least 2 feet wide beside the range, with an adjacent landing surface of heatproof material, either portable or built-in, to accommodate hot pots and pans.

Supply storage nearby for skillets, pans, spoons, and other implements used during cooking. If ovens are separated from the cooktop, plan a heatproof surface for hot dishes coming from the oven.

For safety, it is wise to position a gas range away from windows: otherwise drafts can extinguish the flame, and curtains billowing in the breeze can catch fire.

Combination centers—incorporating two basic work centers—may be the answer if your kitchen space is limited. In combination, two basic centers share the use of one counter. To determine the counter size needed, start with the widest recommended counter of the two centers and then add 1 foot to it. The resulting counter lets both centers function at the same time.

For example, consider combining the refrigerator center and the preparation center. The counter requirement for the refrigerator center is 1½ feet; for the preparation center, 3½ feet. Take the widest counter—the preparation center at 3½ feet—and add 1 foot to it; a counter 4½ feet wide results.

A word of caution: the kitchen designers and researchers who developed the above formula insist that no kitchen should contain less than 10 lineal feet of base storage cabinets. Don't economize on the counters to the extent that needed base cabinets are sacrificed.

Other centers are special

To add new dimension to your kitchen, consider special centers in addition to the four basic ones. Depending on your specific needs and available space, you might incorporate one or more of these centers into your kitchen plan. Keep in mind, though, that these

centers are functional—and therefore worthwhile—only if the tasks they are built for are tasks you perform often.

The most common special centers are a baking center, a beverage bar, a serving or buffet center, a family eating area, an office, and a barbecue. Like the basic centers, these special ones have necessary working surfaces, equipment, appliances, and adequate space to perform specific tasks—all organized into one area.

A baking center suits the cook who specializes in homemade breads and fancy pastries. Most bakers prefer a work surface of wood, laminated plastic, or marble for rolling out and kneading dough. You may wish to have this counter built lower than the others for a better working level. Many cooks like a 32-inch-high counter for stirring and kneading. For further information on counter heights, see page 13.

A counter 30 to 42 inches long is desirable. If a special working surface can't be built into the counter, consider a pull-out board with a surface of wood, a special plastic, or marble. Plan storage for mixers and other appliances, mixing bowls, measuring spoons and cups, and other baking equipment.

You'll also need storage space for flour, sugar, spices, and other ingredients used in baking. One handy solution is tin-lined drawers, ideal for storing large amounts of such frequently used staples as flour and sugar.

If you own a heavy-duty mixer, you may want to install it on a special shelf that swings up into place while the mixer is in use, then retreats into a cabinet for storage.

Several types of baking centers are pictured on pages 68–69.

A bar simplifies parties, but it has everyday uses too, such as routing constant water drinkers away from kitchen work areas. And if sodas, splits, shakes, and sundaes are your forte the bar converts easily to a soda fountain.

Ample glass and bottle storage is essential here. A second sink helps but isn't necessary. If the refrigerator is at a distance, ice storage in the bar area would be convenient; you might even want to consider installing a second refrigerator. If you like to keep a large supply of wine on hand, include wine racks here.

A serving or buffet counter
takes the work out of meal serving. A well-planned area allows table setting, food service, and cleanup without frequent trips from kitchen to dining room, patio, or other eating areas. Ideally, you would situate this center near dish and flatware storage and the cooktop and oven.

To achieve this quick and easy serving center, consider a buffet counter, a pass-through to the dining room or patio, or a serving cart. A combination of these could also work well—using both a pass-through to the patio area and a serving cart to be wheeled into the dining room would handle both areas efficiently.

For easy buffet-style serving, plan a kitchen counter (it could double as an eating counter) located out of major kitchen work areas. Such a counter needs either a heat-proof surface—tile, for example—or portable pads for use under hot dishes. This serving arrangement will work equally well for family meals and large parties.

Try to anticipate possible traffic problems: people should be able to move along the counter and then to the table without any bottlenecks.

A pass-through—perennial and versatile favorite for saving steps—is a hole in the wall, with or without a door, at or above counter level,

Buffet serving counter in dining room is easy to reach from inside kitchen. Pass-through closes with folding doors. Architects: Paul McKim and Associates.

for handing dishes, flatware, linens, and food from one area to another. Pass-throughs work equally well from the kitchen to the dining room or to patio or pool areas. Unlike the buffet counter, a pass-through doesn't subtract from valuable kitchen space.

A serving cart offers the ultimate in mobility—dishes, flatware, and the meal itself can be loaded onto the cart, wheeled to the table, and reloaded after dinner for the return trip. A cart is especially functional in a kitchen where dish storage and cooking facilities are at opposite ends of the kitchen; the cart can be wheeled to various storage areas and work centers for easy loading.

Storing the cart is also an easy matter. A "garage" of undercounter space that the cart rolls into can neatly conceal it. If the cart has a working surface, such as a butcher-block top, give it a parking spot at the end of a counter to add extra working space to the kitchen. Both of these options are pictured on pages 66–67.

A barbecue in the kitchen is a great boon to the family that loves barbecued food.

Special grills available for kitchen installation permit barbecuing to be

moved indoors for year-round enjoyment.

Used in conjunction with a ventilating hood or fan, these grills simulate the effect of meat barbecued over hot coals. Some grills incorporate the fan into the counter unit, freeing space overhead. These grills are usually located near the stove, with necessary equipment stored nearby.

If you plan an indoor, built-in barbecue that uses live coals, be very careful to provide good ventilation; charcoal fumes can be deadly.

Wherever you barbecue—in the kitchen or outdoors on a deck or by a pool—plan a nearby storage cabinet for fuel, long-handled utensils, and other necessary items.

A kitchen eating area takes much of the effort out of day-to-day informal dining. It also provides a pleasant area for after-school or summertime snacking or a midmorning coffee klatch with a neighbor. Counters and small tables are favored for in-the-kitchen meals. Be sure to allow a surface space of 24 by 24 inches for each diner. Chairs or stools need approximately 42 inches maneuvering room. For an average-size eating area allow 6½ by 8 to 9 feet of floor space situated where refrigerator or other appliance doors won't open into the eating area.

An office in the kitchen gives the cook a place to plan menus, organize grocery lists, and handle bills and correspondence. Essentials include a writing surface and a chair, as well as space for cook books, writing supplies, a telephone, and possibly a typewriter. The surface should be large enough to be functional (30 inches long, at least), and desk height—29 to 30 inches. Examples of kitchen offices appear on page 70.

Choosing the ingredients of a successful kitchen

Once you draw up the kitchen plan, consider the details—the separate elements that together make up a successful new kitchen. What type of countertop will serve you best? Which wall and floor coverings are most functional? What is the best height for your counters? Should you consider buying new appliances? How much lighting and ventilation is needed? In this section you'll find information and guidelines that will help take the headaches out of decision-making.

For more detailed product information, inquire at retail stores and manufacturers' showrooms, write to manufacturers, contact manufacturers' trade organizations, call the Home Service Director of your local utility company, or ask questions of the extension services of colleges and universities.

To keep costs down and still not skimp on quality and effect, stick to standard sizes, planning room dimensions and window and door locations to accommodate prefabricated cabinet modules. Avoid materials that must be installed by specialized subcontractors—generally, the more building trades involved, the higher the costs.

Another hidden cost factor is delay—before placing an order, check with your supplier to be certain the material is on hand or easily available.

Don't forget the important differences kitchen accessories can make. Window curtains and blinds, attractive light fixtures, towels, canisters, clocks, chairs and stools, and art can add much to a kitchen's appearance.

Materials for kitchen surfaces

The kitchen is perhaps cleaned more frequently and more thoroughly than any other room in a house, the bathroom being the only contender to this title. For this reason, ease of cleaning and durability should be major factors when you choose the various building materials to be used in your new or remodeled kitchen. Surfaces receiving the most wear are countertops, floors, and walls.

If you're using professional help, consider your architect's or designer's suggestions about building materials. Since these people work constantly with building materials, they see and evaluate a product's strengths and weaknesses. They are also aware of any innovative products.

Countertops offer a great potential for choosing from a wide selection of materials. Ceramic tile and plastic laminate are the most common; wooden butcher block, brushed steel, and marble are other possibilities. Special inserts add versatility to any type of counter, and the ideal kitchen incorporates a combination of these counter types, since different kitchen tasks require specialized surfaces.

The splashback—the wall area between the counter and wall cabinets above—may be finished in the same materials.

Be certain the length, width, and corner angles of the unfinished base cabinets are measured precisely so that the countertop you order will fit exactly.

• *Ceramic tile* comes glazed or unglazed in a wide selection of colors and patterns; for color contrast and easier upkeep, try staining the grout. The tile surface safely accepts hot pots and pans and can stand up to cutting or chopping. It is nonabsorbent (except for some types of quarry tile, which should be sealed), resistant to scratches and stains, easy to clean, and more durable than most other surfaces. A disadvantage is that it isn't easy to work quietly in a kitchen that has ceramic tile counters.

• *Plastic laminate* is a popular and easy-to-clean counter material. It is available in many colors, and the wide selection of patterns includes simulated marble, brick, leather, and wood grain, among many other designs. Usually you have a choice of a self-edged countertop with a right-angle front, or a countertop with a rolled edge at the front and coved at the back. Extreme heat can burn plastic laminate, and it needs some protection to prevent cutting and staining.

• *Butcher block* counters add warmth and interest to kitchens. The surface is fine for cutting as well as for making pastry. But it will burn, cut, and stain, and it will probably need occasional sanding and refinishing.

• *Metal* countertops are useful as inserts near a stove or oven for receiving hot pots and pans. The surface is easily cut and scratched; however, brushed steel camouflages minor abuse.

• *Marble* remains the most elegant counter material. Its beautiful veined surface is impervious to water and heat. If mistreated, though, it will stain, crack, and scratch. Marble is best used as a small insert for pastry and candy making or as a heatproof landing pad near the range or oven.

• *Imitation marble,* a filled polymer, is increasingly available in sheet form for kitchen countertops. Manufactured in several widths and thicknesses, it can be worked much like wood and can be fabricated with power tools (preferably those with carbide edges).

• *Combination* counter surfaces create the most functional kitchen. A wooden butcher block or glass-ceramic insert aids in cutting and chopping foods. A heatproof section of metal, tile, glass-ceramic material, or marble serves as a landing pad for hot pans and pots. Butcher block, glass-ceramic, or marble inserts double as pastry boards.

For greatest efficiency, these counter inserts should be placed as near as possible to the kitchen centers they will serve. Look for further information on kitchen centers on pages 8–11.

Floor coverings most commonly used in kitchens are resilient floor materials and kitchen carpeting. If properly chosen, both surfaces will serve well. Two other options in kitchen flooring are ceramic tile and wood.

• *Resilient* floor coverings come in many forms: linoleum, asphalt tile, vinyl tile, cork tile, sheet vinyl, and floorings that combine some of these materials. Some are cushioned with a foam backing to make them softer underfoot. The newer inlaid sheet vinyls are available with no-wax surfaces—a true timesaver.

The home handyman can lay some of these floorings; others require professional installation. Individual tiles to be cemented and those with an adhesive backing lend themselves to do-it-yourself installation. Sheet floorings are more difficult to install, but easier to maintain because they have fewer seams. Coving sheet flooring up the walls a few inches (where baseboard would normally be used) simplifies sweeping and mopping.

The variables in resilient flooring are cost of materials and installation, durability of materials, amount of care needed, and variety of available colors and patterns.

• *Carpeting* in the kitchen is a fairly recent development. Soft, quiet, and warm, it is available in many colors and patterns. It comes either as wall-to-wall carpeting or carpet tiles; the tiles don't require professional installation. Choose a short, nonsculptured carpet that is durable and stain-resistant.

• *Ceramic tile* for kitchen floors can be either matte-finished, earth-colored quarry tile or glazed tiles in brilliant colors and patterns. Ceramic tile resists marring, burns, stains, and cuts; it doesn't require refurbishing or waxing.

• *Wood* flooring becomes practical for kitchens when it is protected by a sealer that minimizes upkeep. Correctly applied, polyurethane can make a wood floor stain-resistant and virtually waterproof. Some homeowners add area rugs to the wood floors in their kitchens.

Wall coverings used in the kitchen are usually paint or wallpaper. Both provide durable surfaces and can be changed fairly easily for a quick kitchen face lift.

• *Paint* is inexpensive, easy for the homeowner to apply, and available in every color imaginable. You can have paints mixed to create the exact color you want. For an easy-to-clean surface, choose washable paint.

• *Wallpaper* comes in a wide variety of colors and patterns, as well as prices. Be sure the wallpaper you choose is scrubbable, or coat it with plastic yourself. Most wallpapers can be hung by an amateur. For do-it-yourselfers, manufacturers supply prepasted and pretrimmed papers.

Your choices in cabinets

When you're choosing new kitchen cabinets, your main decision is whether to use prefabricated cabinets or have them custom-built by a cabinetmaker. Either way, you'll have a wide choice of materials, styles, and finishes. Take time to inspect both types before making your decision; cabinets represent the largest investment in a new kitchen.

Hardware should be chosen early, especially if cabinets will be custom-built. Pulls, knobs, and hinges come in many materials and styles.

If you're keeping existing cabinets but replacing old knobs and pulls with hardware of a similar type and size, the same holes can be used again. The size is measured from center to center of the holes.

Custom-built cabinets offer the greatest flexibility, since they can be constructed to exact specifications.

Use custom cabinets where there are unusual or difficult structural conditions. Be sure to get several bids and ask for references from previous customers of the cabinetmaker. Custom cabinets can be built on the job or in a cabinet shop. For perfect uniformity, order all your cabinets at the same time.

Those who have the necessary skill and patience can save money by doing their own cabinetmaking. Materials represent only about a fifth of the total cost of professional cabinetwork. And because doing the work yourself makes it so inexpensive, you may find you can afford higher quality materials.

Prefabricated cabinets are less expensive than custom-built ones. They can be constructed of metal, wood, plastic laminate, or a combination of materials.

Since stock cabinets are manufactured in large quantities, sizes have been standardized. Base cabinets are commonly 24 inches deep and 34½ inches high (with a 1½-inch countertop bringing them to the standard 36-inch height). Wall cabinets are generally 12 to 15 inches deep and from 12 to 36 inches high (15, 18, and 30-inch sizes are most commonly used).

Cabinet widths normally start at 9 inches and go to 36 inches in increments of 3 inches. Beyond the 36-inch width, stock cabinets increase in size by 6-inch increments—they are made in 42-inch, 48-inch, 54-inch, and sometimes 60-inch sizes. Filler strips are used to adjust cabinets to fit in an odd-size space. Some prefabricated cabinet companies offer custom-designed cabinets on special order; this will add to the expense.

With standard wall cabinets, there will be space between the top of the units and the ceiling. This space can be enclosed for extra storage, used for light fixtures (soffit lighting, for example), or left open.

When you plan cabinets, exact measurements are essential. Always have your final measurements checked by the supplier before ordering stock cabinets.

For a better fit, filler strips—similar to furring strips, but finished to match cabinetry if they will be visible—can be used on the side of a cabinet that butts against a wall. Rarely is a wall absolutely plumb or free of bumps.

If you want to keep costs down, use the widest possible cabinet to fill the available space, and then add fillers as needed. In other words, use a few wide cabinets rather than many narrow ones.

Unless you are a skilled woodworker, you'll be wise to leave cabinet installation to the experts.

The right counter height

The height of the counters affects the well-being of the cook. A 36-inch counter height is considered average. Manufacturers of drop-in appliances and prefabricated cabinets use this height as a guideline. Built-in dishwashers and drop-in ranges require at least a 36-inch-high counter. However, a separate cooktop unit can be placed in a lowered or raised counter.

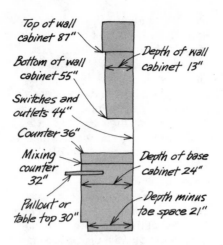

Top of wall cabinet 87"
Bottom of wall cabinet 55"
Switches and outlets 44"
Counter 36"
Mixing counter 32"
Pullout or table top 30"
Depth of wall cabinet 13"
Depth of base cabinet 24"
Depth minus toe space 21"

The short cook may prefer a counter height of 34 inches or less. Lowering just one counter or an island to facilitate chopping and stirring may be enough to alleviate the problem. You can reduce the height of prefabricated cabinets by simply reducing the kick space at the bottom.

The tall cook may wish to raise counters a few inches. Again, a single working surface higher than the standard 36 inches may be sufficient. But if most surfaces are raised, the upper wall cabinets should also be raised to keep the kitchen in proportion.

A general rule of thumb is to put the work surface 3 inches below your elbow joint. However, an even lower surface can ease tasks that require more downward pushing, such as kneading dough.

Keep resale value of your home in mind when you're debating whether or not to alter a kitchen from the norm. Low counters of 32 inches or high ones of 39 inches may severely limit the number of prospective buyers in the future.

Appliances . . . becoming better

Consider new appliances for your new or remodeled kitchen; their timesaving devices and new features may be well worth the extra expense. Keep in mind, though, that the more complex the appliance, the greater the chance of breakdowns.

Size and working requirements of new appliances may dictate their placement, ruling out choices. Check your kitchen measurements carefully and be aware of special appliance operation needs (a water line for a refrigerator with an ice maker, for example) so these can be included in your final layout.

If you want to install a new appliance at minimum expense, have someone who is an expert on installation come and look at your kitchen before you plunge into remodeling. Expect to add extra circuits if you install more appliances than you now have. Local codes may require you to update wiring for the rest of the house at the same time you redo the kitchen circuitry.

Most new appliances come with use and care instructions. Be sure to read the information carefully, following all directions and suggestions to prolong the life and ensure the efficiency of your new appliance.

Kitchen sinks are in constant use, from initial food preparation to final meal cleanup. This is not a place to compromise—since you'll use the sink so much, you should choose exactly what will meet your needs.

Some sinks are constructed of stainless steel. These sinks generally have a brushed surface that camouflages scratches and wear marks. Others are of cast iron or steel coated with porcelain, and come finished in white and a variety of colors.

Single, double, and triple-bowl sinks are available. Single-bowl sinks are usually large enough to hold roasting pans and casseroles. Double-bowl sinks may have both bowls the same size or one larger than the other. A triple-bowl sink permits more than one cook to work at the same time. Sinks also come shaped for corner installation, an arrangement that saves space but is too cramped, generally, to allow two people to work comfortably at the same time. Standard sinks are 24 to 36 inches wide.

Efficient partitioning creates slots for paper bags of various sizes, hanging space for towels, and two bins for assorted cleaning supplies. Architects: Moyer Associates.

A garbage disposer can be put into any type of sink. A shallow bowl containing the disposer is an option for a double-bowl sink; in a triple-bowl unit, a shallow bowl is the standard center sink. Usually the disposer can be installed in either bowl, so it pays to analyze your work habits and decide whether left or right (or center, in a triple-bowl sink) would be more convenient.

Other sink options include dispensers for liquid soap, hand lotion, and instant hot water, as well as pop-up drains, spray attachments, and extended drainboards. Many types of faucets are available in double or single-lever styles.

Dishwashers are the biggest time-savers in any modern kitchen. Models come built-in, convertible, or portable; they may be top or front-loading. Some contain soft food disposers that eliminate the need for careful prerinsing. Most models provide adjustable shelves

for easy loading. More expensive models have a variety of cycles that handle cleaning jobs from extra dirty pots and pans to fragile china and crystal.

Standard built-in types either slip underneath a continuous countertop or display their own top style and material. Some models include reversible front and side color panels so you can change colors later, if you wish.

A built-in dishwasher can be placed near the center of a kitchen counter, at the end, or in a peninsula. Most often, a dishwasher is placed to the left of the sink, but if you are left-handed you may prefer it on the right.

It is possible to remove a base cabinet next to the sink and install a dishwasher in its place (most dishwashers are 24 inches wide). But confer with a plumber to see whether the machine can be installed where you want it to go. Usually the store where you purchase the dishwasher can do the installation, but you may have to consult a plumber. Either way, you may need to find your own electrician and carpenter.

Garbage disposers grind up most soft food wastes. Many models are sturdy enough to handle such tough garbage as fruit pits, celery, and corn husks.

The two main types of disposers are batch-feed and continuous-feed. The continuous-feed disposer allows you to add scraps as the unit is grinding. This type requires a separate wall switch. As a precautionary measure, be sure the on/off switch is out of a child's reach. The batch-feed disposes of one load at a time; the cover is the switch control.

Trash compactors, relative newcomers, reduce dry household waste to a fraction of its normal size, cutting down on trash volume. (This appliance does not replace a garbage disposer; it is best to avoid placing wet garbage in a compactor.) Some compactors come with attachments to control odor. If you have a large family or more than

average amounts of trash, consider including a compactor in your kitchen plan.

Most trash compactors fit the same space as a standard 15-inch-wide kitchen cabinet and can be built in under the counter or used as a freestanding unit. They operate from an electric outlet.

Refrigerator/freezers feature self-defrosting models in addition to the standard manual defrost type. Though this option is a definite timesaver, it uses more energy.

For keeping meats and fresh produce, special compartments are available, some with individual temperature controls. Many models contain adjustable shelves for more efficient storage. Ice makers and cold water dispensers are convenience features.

Experts usually calculate a minimum of 6 to 8 cubic feet of refrigerator space for a family of two, then add 1 cubic foot for each additional person.

A single-door refrigerator usually contains a frozen food compartment; such a compartment is not for long-term freezer storage (see owner's manual for specific information). In refrigerator/freezer combinations, each unit has an individual door; they can be vertical side-by-side compartments or ones in which the horizontal freezer is located at the top or bottom. This type of freezer is safe for long-term storage. Doors can be hinged from either side to fit your kitchen layout.

Refrigerators can be built-in or freestanding; they come in a variety of sizes. Refrigerators typically are 25 inches deep; widths vary with capacity, but 30 or 36 inches is typical. Auxiliary under-counter small refrigerators are available. Separate freezers come in chest or upright models.

Refrigerators are easy appliances to install—most just need to be plugged in. Models featuring an automatic ice maker or cold water dispenser, though, must be connected to water pipes.

Fit can be a problem, so measure the refrigerator to an eighth of an inch and be sure to measure height. Many new models do not require extra space to open the door, so can fit almost flush into a corner or at the end of a row of cabinets. It is advisable, though, to allow ½ to 1 inch on the sides and at the top for easy installation and for air circulation.

If you want to build in a refrigerator, you must use a model designed especially for this purpose.

Ranges, cooktops, and ovens offer you many options. You can select a gas or electric freestanding range, slide-in range, or built-in range, perhaps with two ovens or a microwave oven included. Or you can team a built-in cooktop with separate wall ovens.

Freestanding ranges that rest on the floor offer the widest assortment of prices, sizes, and features. The high-oven range is a freestanding model with a built-in look. A slide-in range is a variation of the freestanding range: it is self-contained and rests on the floor, but the sides are unfinished and it fits snugly between base cabinets. A drop-in or built-in range is like the slide-in, except it rests on the cabinet base or a specially constructed unit, not the floor.

The easiest and least expensive way to replace a range is to use a slip-in or freestanding model close in width to your old one. Don't switch fuels arbitrarily—going from gas to electricity or vice versa can be costly.

With a self-cleaning oven, you can forget ammonia fumes and broken fingernails. There are two types of oven cleaning systems available both in range and wall ovens—self cleaning (or pyrolitic) and continuous cleaning (or catalytic). The pyrolitic system uses a separate, timed, high-temperature cycle to burn off residue. The catalytic

Commercial gas range *with built-in griddle is highlight of kitchen remodel. Architect: Linda Ludden Mathews.*

system cleans as the oven bakes at normal temperatures. Large spills must still be removed manually in the continuous-cleaning system.

Other optional range and oven features include removable parts for easy cleaning, food warmers, meat thermometers, rotisseries, and elaborate timers. Oven doors often have glass panels so you can watch the baking process. In some models, you can customize oven doors by using a door paneling kit.

Cooktop options are barbecue grills, griddles, and rotisseries. Some cooktops contain a built-in fan that eliminates the need for overhead ventilation. However, this type must be ducted to the outside. (For further information on kitchen ventilation, see pages 16–17.)

Smooth glass-ceramic surface cooktops can double as work space when you aren't cooking; they are durable and unaffected by temperature changes, and cleaning up spilled food from them is easy. However, they heat somewhat more slowly than open flame or electric coil, certain substances stain them permanently, and flat-bottomed pots and pans must be used for best cooking results.

Freestanding ranges vary from 20 to 42 inches wide; slide-in

ranges measure from 20 to 36 inches wide; a drop-in or built-in range is usually 30 inches wide. Cooktops have two or four cooking units on a 12 to 42-inch base. Wall ovens vary from 24 to 30 inches wide; capacity varies accordingly.

Microwave ovens—among the newest kitchen appliances—are ideal for busy families who eat on the run or at several different times, since meals cooked in a microwave oven can be prepared in minutes.

The cooking principle of a microwave oven is totally different from that of a conventional oven. Cooking is accomplished through electromagnetic waves generated from a magnetron tube. These waves are either reflected, transmitted, or absorbed—metals reflect them; glass, paper, and most plastics transmit them; food absorbs them. Microwaves enter food and cause its moisture molecules to vibrate rapidly; the friction created results in heat energy that cooks the food. The air around the food remains cool.

Microwave ovens are easy to clean because spills don't burn onto the oven surfaces. Utensils to cook in can be almost anything but metal—even a paper plate!

Microwave ovens can be portable countertop models, built-in units, or part of a complete range containing two ovens—one microwave, one conventional.

Because of possibly dangerous leakage of microwaves, all microwave ovens must meet stringent safety requirements. Ovens need at least two separate interlocks to shut off energy whenever the door is opened. Special door construction must keep radiant energy leakage to a level considered negligible.

Though microwave cooking does have limitations (foods such as steak or chops will not brown without a built-in browner or separate browning unit) and a microwave oven probably won't replace your conventional oven, it does thaw frozen foods, heat leftovers, and cook a wide variety of foods quickly.

Electrical wiring

Your kitchen requires three types of wiring: 1) general purpose circuits for lighting, 2) branch circuits for small appliances, and 3) individual branch circuits for such major appliances as an electric range or a dishwasher.

Locate the branch outlets for small appliances carefully. Above-counter outlets should be about 3 or 4 feet apart, unless a continuous strip system is used. Or you can provide hidden outlets in the cabinetry so appliances remain plugged in all the time.

Wiring specifications may vary from city to city, depending on local codes. Check with your local building department for additional wiring and electrical information. Check, too, with your utility company—some offer free analysis and recommendations for home lighting and wiring needs.

Lighting the kitchen

Good kitchen lighting depends on illuminating the kitchen as a whole, plus spotlighting specific work areas. Proper lighting allows meal preparation and cleanup without causing eyestrain. Natural light from windows and skylights is ideal, but it must be supplemented with well-planned electrical lighting.

Overall lighting should provide glare-free, shadowless light on all floor areas and traffic paths. Common fixtures for general lighting are individual ceiling units or large ceiling panels of a translucent material.

A good rule of thumb for determining size and wattage for ceiling light fixtures is to allow one fixture, containing 175 to 250 watts incandescent or 60 to 80 watts fluorescent light, for every 50 square feet of area. If suspended luminous ceiling fixtures are used, provide 2 watts incandescent or ¾ to 1 watt fluorescent light for each square foot of kitchen area.

The height of the ceiling and the color of the kitchen will also affect the overall lighting—white and light colors reflect light; darker colors tend to absorb it. A kitchen in dark wood tones, for example, requires more general lighting than a pale yellow room. And a high-ceilinged kitchen would need more lighting than a low-ceilinged one.

You can focus light on specific work areas in a number of ways: incandescent or fluorescent lighting under cabinets; spotlights on the ceiling or under a soffit; light units in a hood; individual fixtures positioned over a major work area, such as the sink.

Fluorescent lighting with warm-toned tubes is often recommended for kitchen use. Tubes disperse light more evenly than bulbs; they are especially valuable for eliminating shadows under wall cabinets. Fluorescent lights use less energy and last longer than incandescent ones, but their blue-white color is harsher than more yellowish, sun-like incandescent light. Consequently, special warm-toned fluorescent tubes are a good compromise.

Over the sink or range, provide 150 to 200 watts incandescent or 60 watts fluorescent light. Counters are often lighted by one 20-watt fluorescent tube for every 3 feet of counter length, with a shielding device if tubes are mounted against the wall or in line of vision. For a kitchen eating area, plan a minimum of 150 watts incandescent light for dining.

If you plan to add a number of new light fixtures, have wiring checked to be sure your present electrical system is adequate. Your utility company may have information suggesting bulb types and wattages for specific locations.

Ventilating your kitchen

Nothing can be worse than the cooking odors of last night's liver. A good ventilation system removes unpleasant odors, steam, grease, and excessive heat—all the necessary evils that cooking creates.

Locate ventilating fans as near to the stove or cooktop as possible (usually 21 to 30 inches above it) for greatest efficiency. A ceiling fan must be powerful enough to draw up odors, heat, and grease. A relatively inexpensive wall fan installed directly over the stove would do a fairly good job of ventilating.

Some cooktops incorporate a fan right on the cooktop unit, drawing grease and heat down instead of upward.

The draft of an overhead fan will be increased if the fan is in a hood, which also helps to protect adjacent cabinets from smoke. The perimeter of a stove hood should be

Built into ventilating hood, fold-down rack keeps casserole near heat.

slightly greater than that of the cooktop; its bottom rim should be 18 to 36 inches above the surface units to allow for head clearance.

Two basic types of ventilating fans are available—ducted and nonducted—with various grades, prices, sizes, styles, and colors of hoods to choose from. With a ducted system, venting to the outside by the shortest and most direct route keeps efficiency up.

The performance of ducted ventilating fans is rated on the basis of the number of cubic feet of air removed per minute (CFM). The Home Ventilating Institute recommends a range hood with a minimum capacity of 40 CFM per linear foot when placed along the wall and 50 CFM per linear foot for peninsula or island ranges.

By multiplying the number of square feet of kitchen floor space by two, you can determine the CFM rating required for 15 air changes an hour in your kitchen. Often, code requirements set minimum CFM ratings.

Ducting the exhaust out of the house can be tricky, especially if your range or cooktop is located on an interior wall or on an island. Be guided by your architect, contractor, or ventilation specialist.

If it isn't possible to duct the fan outside, you can use a ductless ventilating hood fan, though such fans are much less efficient. Ductless range hoods circulate air through replaceable filters, helping to remove unpleasant odors, smoke, and grease—but not heat or moisture.

Ventilating fans certified by the Home Ventilating Institute have a sound rating (measured in sones) as well as an air-movement rating. The limit for a kitchen fan (up to 500 CFM) is eight sones.

Because the kitchen usually generates more heat and moisture than any other room, a room air conditioner may be desirable if the house isn't centrally air conditioned.

Planning storage

What could be more important than proper storage in the kitchen? For sheer numbers of items to be put away, no other room even comes close to the kitchen.

Specific storage in kitchen centers is discussed on pages 8–11. Additional types of specialized storage are illustrated on pages 68–79.

Existing storage areas can be supplemented with commercially available units. Standard-size drawers, bins, shelves, turntables, and special racks can be found in housewares sections of department or hardware stores. These units can store an assortment of such hard-to-place items as pan lids, spice jars, and prepared foods.

Frequently used items—pots and pans, table linens, spices and herbs, canned goods and packaged foods, small appliances, and trash containers—need specialized storage that is easily accessible. Several ideas for storing each of these items are pictured on pages 68–79. You can probably adapt some of these suggestions in your own kitchen planning.

Storing equipment, utensils, food, and supplies close to their point of first use saves time. It's often a good idea to duplicate items that are frequently used at two or more of the work centers.

Remember that everyday items should be close at hand, and the area between waist and eye level is most efficient for storage. Seldom-used items can be placed where you have to bend or stretch to reach them. For persons of average height, the things most often used should be stored no more than 72 inches from the floor—or within fingertip reach as you stand behind a 25-inch-deep counter.

Getting the job done

Once you've come up with the answers to what you want in your new kitchen, it's time to cope with the question of how you'll get the job done.

Should you hire an architect or a kitchen designer to design and draw up the detailed plans? Or would you rather do all the planning and drafting yourself? Should you use a contractor? How much of the actual work, if any, should you do yourself? These decisions will greatly affect the cost and timetable—and perhaps the final outcome—of your new or remodeled kitchen.

If your kitchen project is part of a new house, you may find that planning and carrying out the construction is much easier than if you were remodeling an existing kitchen. You won't have to do demolition work; you won't be bound by existing conditions; and you will probably already have the services of an architect and/or contractor.

For these reasons the information in this section focuses on kitchen remodeling. Much of it also applies, though, to the constructing of a brand-new kitchen.

You may choose to do a kitchen remodeling project in stages to avoid spending a lot of money all at once, but doing a kitchen in stages generally ends up costing more in the long run. And you'll be coping with a dismantled kitchen over and over again.

Your own role

Whether you take a do-it-yourself approach, turn the entire job over to professionals, or work out a plan somewhere in between, you will play a key role in making everything work smoothly.

Advice for do-it-yourselfers: if you wish to do part or all of the job yourself, be sure you are well qualified for the various tasks. Most remodeling projects will have to meet local building code specifications. Some jobs—laying resilient floor tiles, hanging wallpaper, and painting walls and cabinets, for example —are easy for the average handyman. Others, such as plumbing, electrical work, and cabinet construction, are often best left to skilled workmen.

If you want to do a substantial part of the work yourself, refer to the following list of chronological steps:

1) Measure the kitchen to determine the total space available (for accuracy, use a carpenter's 8-foot folding ruler with slide-out extension).

2) Draw a floor plan to scale (see page 8).

3) Determine approximate locations for the main work centers.

4) Determine approximate locations for any specialized centers.

5) Plan a detailed layout showing the exact position of each appliance and cabinet, along with breakfast table and chairs, planning desk, and other features, and superimpose that layout on the floor plan.

6) Write an outline briefly describing the work to be done.

7) Make a list of all materials and equipment necessary for the job.

8) Order materials and equipment.

9) Hire subcontractors, if any.

10) Set up a work schedule with the subcontractors.

None of the actual work begins until you've taken all the steps in the planning stage and—just as important—until all materials and supplies are at hand.

Once you're past the planning stage and ready to begin construction, the work proceeds in the following order (though some steps may not apply, depending on how extensive the project is): disconnect all appliances, remove cabinets and countertops, and take up flooring and any wall tiles. Make any structural changes such as relocating doors and windows. Repair walls and subflooring as necessary, rough in plumbing connections, and relocate electrical switches, outlets, wiring, and light fixtures. Install new equipment and connect new appliances. Finish the walls and install new flooring.

A temporary kitchen elsewhere in the house will help avert chaos. You can plug the refrigerator into any convenient electric outlet—in the dining room or another room on the same floor as the kitchen. In summer, you could even set up your temporary kitchen outside on a deck or patio.

To cook, take advantage of your portable electric appliances—frying pan, slow cooker, or wok. A small barbecue, fondue pot, or camp stove will also help.

Dishes are perhaps the messiest problem in a torn-up kitchen. Laundry sinks and bathtubs can be commandeered for interim dishwashing—just remember they don't have a garbage disposer built in.

Ease the experts' work by doing everything possible in the way of preparation, even if you're employing a contractor to take over the entire project.

Appliances, cabinets, and construction materials will be delivered to your house a few days before they are actually needed, and you'll have to prepare a place to store them.

Take everything off the walls and remove furniture and anything else that might get in the workmen's way. Everything in the kitchen cabinets must be stored elsewhere. Don't forget to unscrew towel racks, can openers, and similar items; take down curtains, blinds, rods, and brackets. In rooms adjoining the kitchen, you can protect carpeting with plastic drop cloths.

Special arrangements usually have to be made for removal and disposal of old stoves, plasterboard, and other items. Disposing of even the general debris that accumulates during demolition and construction can be a surprisingly difficult and costly undertaking. Find out from the contractor, in advance, how debris removal will be handled. If it is to be your responsibility, consider hiring a scavenger service or obtain a dumping permit.

Permits you may need are a building department permit for structural alterations, a plumbing permit, and an electrical underwriters' permit.

Sometimes a homeowner must have plans executed by a registered architect to obtain a building permit. In some areas all changes in plumbing (with minor exceptions) must be done by a licensed plumber, and in some towns all electrical work with the exception of low-voltage bell wiring must be done by a licensed electrician.

In most cases, work not approved by the electrical inspector and the underwriters' laboratories may partially or totally void a fire insurance policy. But rules, codes, and ordinances vary widely in different parts of the country, and you'll need to check with the building department in your own community.

Contracts and other papers pertaining to your kitchen remodeling project—including credit application forms and promissory notes—should be carefully kept. Use a signed copy of the specifications as a check list to see whether all materials and equipment agreed upon have been delivered and the work specified has actually been done. Check the floor plan against the specifications and try to visualize how the completed kitchen will look, for any changes made after work has begun are almost certain to be expensive and time-consuming—inconveniencing all involved.

Be sure any contract with an architect, designer, or contractor states the approximate kitchen completion date; procedures for breaking the contract or making changes and corrections; terms of payment; and length of warranty on the work.

For major projects, consider an architect or designer

If construction or remodeling will be extensive, carefully consider the advantages of using an architect or kitchen designer. The experience these professionals have had in kitchen planning and building procedures can prevent expensive errors and give you a better kitchen. You can hire them just to prepare detailed blueprints of the kitchen, or you can give them the authority to supervise the entire job.

To find a good architect or designer, rely on personal recommendations. Most architects and kitchen designers are listed in the Yellow Pages of your local telephone book. It's always wise to contact several and ask for references from former clients.

Some large department stores, cabinet shops, building supply and lumber dealers, and plumbing, heating, and electrical companies will handle a complete kitchen remodeling job—including the design stage. They may subcontract such specialized work as masonry or sheet-metal work. As a rule, they prefer simpler projects to more elaborate ones.

Even if you decide to design the kitchen yourself, you'll need to provide a detailed blueprint for the contractor and/or workmen, and it is advisable to consult an architect about your final drawings.

Hiring a contractor

If you decide to hire a contractor to oversee kitchen construction, ask several contractors for competitive bids. The bidding should be based on detailed, building department-approved plans and specifications outlining the materials and equipment that will be used.

Don't hesitate to ask contractors for references. Whenever possible, examine their workmanship on jobs for former clients.

In your specifications, be sure to supply complete information about each kitchen element. Include brand name, manufacturer's name, color, and model. Specify who will supply each item, install it, and do the finishing. And don't forget to state who will do the demolition work.

Painting, wallpapering, and installation of new floor material are not usually included in an agreement with a contractor. You can hire specialists or do the work yourself.

Acting as your own contractor

You can save money by acting as your own contractor—performing some labor yourself and subcontracting the more difficult jobs, or subcontracting all the work. This means more work on your part, and the job will probably take more time.

If you act as your own contractor you should send a set of blueprints with written specifications to each prospective subcontractor. The bidder should visit your home to see the job before he bids. Experience has shown that an hourly labor rate usually ends up costing more than a bid on the job as a whole.

If the job and your community require them, you will need to obtain local permits and schedule inspections as work is completed.

Draw up a schedule for completing each stage of the work and see that the workmen and the materials arrive at the right time.

If you'll be buying a quantity of building supplies from one outlet, ask about a possible discount.

Examples: Kitchens worth a second look

What would it take to make your ideal kitchen a reality? Whether your remodeling plans and needs are simple or extensive, you'll discover new ideas from seeing how other homeowners, designers, and architects have solved different kitchen problems.

First to appear in this chapter are remodeled kitchens. Use the before and after floor plans to help you understand the ways in which each kitchen has been altered. The text describes the remodeling project in more detail.

Later in the chapter come the brand-new kitchens. These examples may come tantalizingly close to your ideal kitchen. Surprisingly, though, many of these were done on a tight budget, and the ways the owners saved money—yet got all the kitchen they wanted—are outlined in the text.

You can use this chapter as a reference in getting to know what options there are—in many areas of kitchen design. For example, you could go through it with an eye for various types of ceiling construction or lighting or storage or countertop material—or just to help you select a color scheme.

At left is pictured a kitchen in which every inch counts—the situation in many houses. It's a small, efficient kitchen where the cook can prepare a meal without logging miles walking from refrigerator to stove to sink.

And for a one-counter kitchen it contains a surprising amount of storage. An entire wall of adjustable open shelves provides storage space from floor to ceiling. En-

closed cabinets and lots of stacked drawers supplement the shelves.

The sink (with its dechromed hospital faucet—distinctive and easy to operate) is the pivotal control point in this kitchen. Wood chopping block counters edge it; the burners are just a short distance away.

The window over the sink lets the cook enjoy a view; it's practical, too, for ventilation. A recess created by a projecting wall conceals the refrigerator, making the kitchen even more trim looking.

This functional kitchen gains glamour with the addition of antique leaded glass cupboard doors. Framed watercolors brighten the white walls. Clerestory windows behind and above the rough-sawn open beams bring natural light into the kitchen.

Architect: Herbert D. Kosovitz.

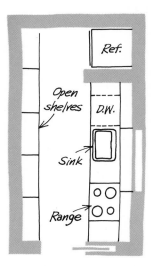

Redefining space sets the stage for efficiency

Around stainless-steel sink, *everything is both easy to reach and pleasant to look at. On open shelf above sink, attractive bowls keep dishwashing supplies at hand but out of sight. While standing in front of the sink, owner can pivot from dishwasher to dish cupboard.*

One of the keys to this kitchen's finely detailed efficiency is the strategically situated open storage. Slots for plates, compartments for serving dishes, and cubbyholes for spices store things just a reach away from where they're used.

All the edges and joints in this kitchen meet—with exceptional precision. The owners describe the kitchen as having been "machined" for efficiency in a small space.

Appropriate storage surrounds each activity center. For example, the drawer beneath the ovens holds baking gear; wide, deep shelves beneath the cooktop hold casseroles and saucepans.

Among its several purposes, the counter peninsula extending out from the wall separates the cooking space from the bar equipment on the other side. Sometimes the family stands around the peninsula while enjoying a quick snack.

Widely varying lighting levels and directions create a range of kitchen moods. Adjustable track lights, undercounter area lights, and indirect lights inset in the tops of the wall cabinets combine for many effects.

Designer: Diana Crawford of Donald Sandy Jr., AIA, James A. Babcock.

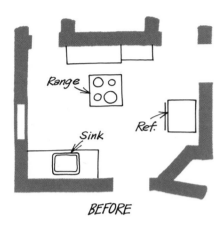

Range
Ref.
Sink

BEFORE

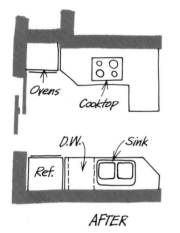

Ovens
Cooktop
D.W.
Sink
Ref.

AFTER

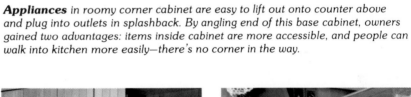

Appliances *in roomy corner cabinet are easy to lift out onto counter above and plug into outlets in splashback. By angling end of this base cabinet, owners gained two advantages: items inside cabinet are more accessible, and people can walk into kitchen more easily—there's no corner in the way.*

Peninsula counter *includes auxiliary refrigerator, series of drawers. One side of peninsula stores kitchen-oriented items; other side contains entertaining supplies. Dividers in bottom drawer separate lids, pie and flan pans.*

Well-thought-out storage in a family kitchen

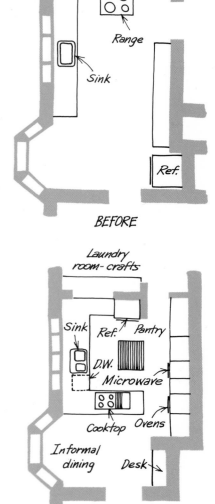

BEFORE

AFTER

White-tiled counters and light walls brighten kitchen, accent handsome oak cabinets. Built-in spice and condiment storage lets baker measure teaspoon of salt without bringing out and putting away awkward packages.

Pass-through between kitchen and laundry room has vertical sliding panel that is a blackboard on laundry room side of the wall.

When this family decided to remodel their kitchen, they began by mentally "putting away" everything they used in the kitchen.

The result is a tightly organized, easy-to-work-in family kitchen. One of the main contributors to its tidy look is a continuous row of compartments, concealed behind sliding panels, running above the counter that surrounds the sink. These compartments hide—but keep handy—the inelegant things that need to be used daily. In the compartment nearest the breakfast area, for example, a toaster and waffle iron are hidden away.

The center island houses a swing up platform that brings a mixer to counter level. Beyond the island is a solid wall of cupboards, cabinets, and drawers (photograph on page 68), punctuated by inset double conventional ovens and a microwave oven.

Between the kitchen and the breakfast area, overhead cupboards

are extra deep—they measure about 2½ feet. One end of the row of cupboards stores food; the other hides holiday supplies. Another row of overhead cupboards on the opposite side of the kitchen hangs extra high so that adults can reach what's in them and children can't.

The peninsula between the kitchen and the breakfast area houses shallow shelves and drawers on the breakfast area side. On the kitchen side, oversize drawers underneath the cooktop store pots and pans.

Architects: Moyer Associates.

New island rejuvenates aging kitchen

Cooperative cooking *uses new island to fullest. Three overhead lamps help cooks see what they're doing. Shelf across window holds houseplant array.*

Empty floor space that gave the cook an unnecessary amount of exercise was replaced by a new cooking island. Three blue lamps overhead shine plenty of light down on what's cooking.

The island solves a traffic problem: it diverts people away from the action in the work triangle as they walk through the kitchen to the back door or back stairs. Removing excess doors also helped make this kitchen an efficient work room.

Base cabinets of vertical-grain fir are new; wall cabinets were retained and painted white. The bright blue backsplash and shelf recesses add color interest that is repeated in functional accessories.

Architects: Sortun-Cahill-Granger.

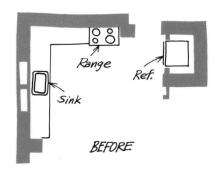

BEFORE

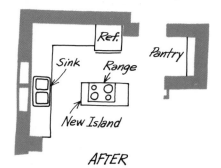

AFTER

Basketball player *ducks into refrigerator for quick glass of milk. Plant ledges fill blue-painted ironing board niche; open pantry shelves occupy another bright blue recess.*

Streamlined kitchen remodeled around center-of-activity island

Open areas above cabinets let cook enjoy plants, give kitchen airy, spacious feeling. Desk in foreground functions as message, communications center.

The centered, rectangular, butcher block-topped island separates activity zones in this remodeled kitchen. On one side of the island are the sink and refrigerator; across the island is a complete array of cooking equipment. A built-in desk attaches to the end of the island beyond a raised and tiled divider that visually separates the kitchen from the informal eating area.

In the course of remodeling, the best parts of the original kitchen were retained—a ventilating hood of stainless steel, the cooktop location, a built-in barbecue, and the slate floor.

The two most important changes—other than the new dark-stained cabinets and the addition of the island—were the extension of the eating area to provide more space and take advantage of the eye-stopping view, and the addition of more cooking machinery.

A full range of cooking facilities lines up in an L around the island. A gas cooktop with conventional burners, an electric cooktop with two burners and a griddle, a built-in barbecue, conventional double wall ovens, a microwave oven, and a warming oven encourage ambitious cooking projects.

To prepare a complete meal, the cook starts at the refrigerator and proceeds around the island. The island itself provides an expanse of work space—butcher block to chop on plus a marble insert to prepare candy or pastry on. Lots of cabinets, pull-out shelves, and special drawers make the island a centralized storage resource, too.

Architect: Thaddeus E. Kusmierski.

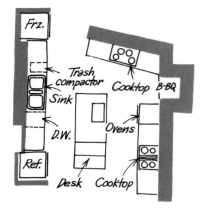

Greenhouse

Greenhouse wall *frames view in remodeled and extended eating area. Previously, bank of cabinets blocked view, and family ate at a counter.*

Striking *stainless-steel backsplash and hood highlight L-shaped cooking area. Island's marble insert speeds pastry making.*

Glide-out drawers *above dishwasher can also be reached from dining room on other side of this wall.*

Vaulted ceiling, colorful window make kitchen seem big

Busy focus of kitchen activity, low island harbors serving cart. Butcher-block top stands up to heavy use. Well-stocked pantry is conveniently close to island.

Chortling baby splashes away in single-basin kitchen sink. This type of large sink can serve multiple duty for hand laundry or flower arranging, as well as for baby bathing and customary kitchen work at the sink.

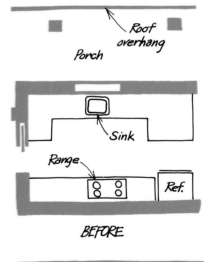

BEFORE

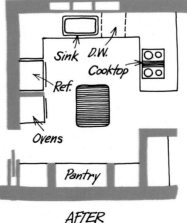

AFTER

Raising the ceiling and installing a dramatic stained-glass window transformed this rather small kitchen into a unique place to work. The high window, used instead of a skylight, brings in plenty of west light.

This family gathers in the kitchen—all the children help with dinner. For this reason, the kitchen had first priority both on the list of house remodeling projects and in the use of available space. To gain more kitchen space, the owners decided to extend the front wall of the house out beyond a seldom-used porch.

Chief cooks and helpers center their activities around the island. Low enough for bread-making, it conceals a cart that is wheeled out to a deck for serving summer meals. The big pantry provides more than enough storage, and the cooktop on a peninsula is handy to the informal eating area. Plenty of counter space aids in the cooperative mealtime efforts.

The owner finds the counters of white ceramic tile with dark grout to be very practical. Butcher block on the center island supplements the tile counters.

Pull-out shelves for pots and pans and curved, lipped shelves attached to cabinet doors supplement storage. Shallow cabinets on the eating area side of the cooktop peninsula store tableware. Vertical dividers separate trays and cookie sheets in the cabinet above the wall ovens.

Architects: Moyer Associates.

Now the whole family enjoys the kitchen

In this added-on kitchen, the most decorative, attractive features are also the most functional ones. The rich blue tile resists heat and scratches; the handsome island forms the pivot point for cooking chores; the gleaming copper rack holds working pots directly above the cooktop.

The island's raised sides serve several purposes. Most importantly, they are a safety barrier between the cooktop and children moving around the kitchen. In addition, the extended surfaces create valuable extra work counters. Hot pans can be lifted off the burners and set down directly on the tile. Ingredients can be organized and ready to use, adjacent to the cooktop, yet up out of the way.

Around the sink, chores flow in an easy sequence. Flanking the sink, the oak-fronted dishwasher and trash compactor are at arm's length. Wooden chopping blocks built into the counters adjacent to the sink position slicing and mincing chores in logical spots. And the large cabinet beyond the trash compactor holds recycling bins.

One goal of the owners when adding on the kitchen was to carry over the architectural feeling of the rest of the 1920s house. The window style, wood framing and molding, and wood floors help accomplish this goal.

Wanting all members of their family to be together in this new kitchen, the owners planned space enough for everyone. The counter with a cutout underneath for stools, intended as a children's work area, functions as an eating counter, too. And at the island, one person can sit on a stool and kibitz or grate cheese while another cooks.

Speakers in the wall above the refrigerator and ovens send music through the kitchen.

For another view of this kitchen, see the cover photograph.

Architect: George W. Seitz.

Open underneath, end of island conceals handy stool (to be replaced eventually by a serving cart). Because small children can reach into them, drawers built into island hold such harmless things as hot pads and foil.

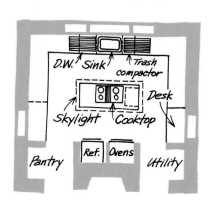

Children's counter lets youngsters measure, mix their own favorites.

Double-door pantry between kitchen and sitting room holds boxes and cans on shelves attached to doors, as well as on adjustable shelves inside pantry.

An interior room flooded with light

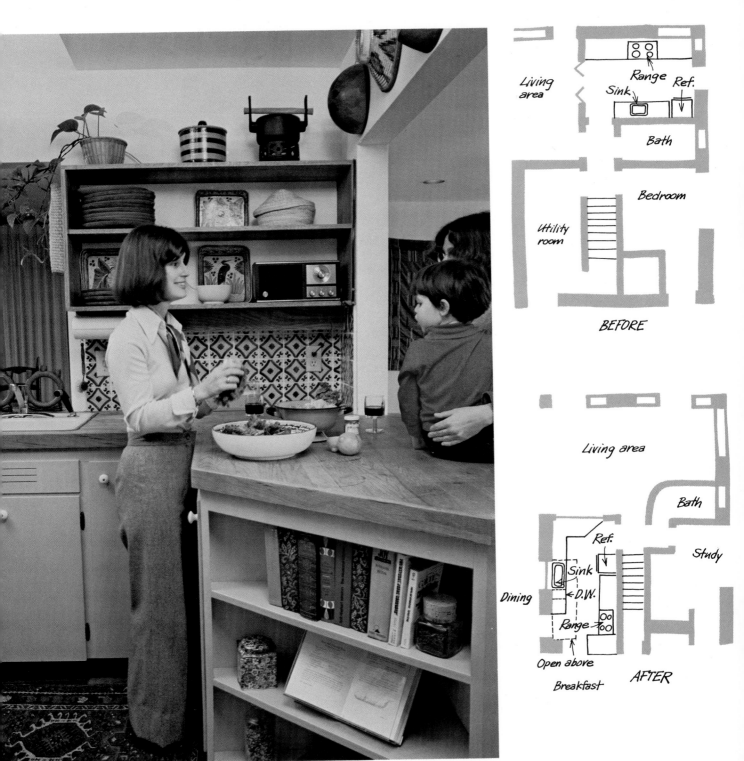

Living area

Range **Ref.**

Sink

Bath

Bedroom

Utility room

BEFORE

Living area

Bath

Ref.

Study

Sink

Dining

D.W.

Range

Open above

Breakfast

AFTER

Opened up *on four sides and overhead, kitchen allows views and communication in several directions. Over sink is pass-through to dining room; through opening to right is living room. Angled end of base cabinets makes it easier to enter kitchen; shelves store cook book collection.*

Fresh coat of paint *gave kitchen cabinets new look. Open shelf displays, decorative tile add distinction.*

When the owners and architect decided to move this kitchen from an outside, windowed corner into an interior utility room, they worried about sacrificing an outstanding view and natural light to location priorities. But by opening up three walls and the ceiling, too, they succeeded in bringing light into what might have been a dark, boxy utility-room-turned-kitchen.

Before they could install the kitchen, they had to jack up parts of the house floor. Then they made openings in four directions—to create two pass-throughs (one to the living room, another to the dining room), a walkway and counter on the breakfast room side, and, overhead, a connection to the second story skylight.

The owners did a large percentage of the work themselves to keep costs down. They even took apart the existing kitchen cabinets and re-assembled, rearranged, and re-

painted them in the new space, adding new hardware where required. Installing open shelving, rather than cabinets with doors, for above-counter storage reduced costs. Reusing appliances also helped keep expenses in line, as did using oiled oak flooring for the countertops.

Architect: Richard Cardwell.

Raised trapezoidal ceiling *leads up to skylight. Long strip of window above counter lets additional daylight into remodeled kitchen painted with primary colors.*

Need more room? Remove a wall

Like many older houses, this one had a wall separating the kitchen and breakfast area. The architect of this kitchen removed the separating wall and, by rearranging cabinets and appliances, brought in more light and provided more storage and open space.

Now that the old wall is gone, a bigger area can take advantage of available light. The skylight over the breakfast table once illuminated only the kitchen—now it brightens the former breakfast area, as well. And tearing out the old wall also made room for another window over the sink counter.

The old range was removed to allow for a new door between the kitchen and bedrooms. A new cooktop was built into the counter near the sink, and an oven replaced the refrigerator in an alcove that also houses a pantry. The refrigerator was moved into the kitchen work triangle, adjacent to the counter and sink. Result: An efficient work area was created with few changes in existing wiring and plumbing.

Since the room is too narrow for ordinary storage cabinets along both walls, very shallow shelves were installed on one wall. They serve as display racks for cups, glasses, and plates. A piece of wood trim forms a lip on the upper shelves to hold glasses and cups in place. Nearby, pots and pans hang flat from hooks attached to perforated particle board panels on the wall.

The shelves on the opposite wall are of typical width (12 inches). A 1 by 2-inch oak strip forms an "earthquake bar" to protect the ceramic dishes handcrafted by the owner. All shelves are open—a condition that displays the dishes and leaves no doors to bump heads on.

Architect: Robert Herman.

Red oak table's base doubles as storage compartment. Narrow open shelving along wall displays glasses, cups, and other dishes; wooden protective edging holds them in place.

Boldly painted built-in ironing board cabinet has new eye appeal.

Around-the-corner pantry has its own skylight. Pull-out board next to wall oven adds surface to set casseroles and baking dishes on.

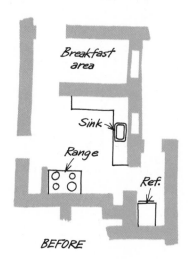

BEFORE

AFTER

Small kitchen shows off window collection

Movable butcher block, brought from owners' previous home, supplements counter space. Window above sink was part of original house; skylights are new.

Antique glass panels on cabinet doors and in a row of skylights add color and atmosphere to this small remodeled kitchen. The wine-colored tile picks up one of the colors in the glass; oak cabinets fitted with teak pulls supply a rich background.

The floor, counter surfaces, and splashbacks are all wine-colored tile, and the tiled toe space extends all the way around the kitchen, creating an encircling band of color. White walls set off the colorful tile and patterned glass.

The built-in breakfast table is an extension of the kitchen base cabinets. The change in levels from kitchen counter to kitchen table created hideaways for a handy telephone and salt and pepper shakers, plus an electrical outlet. Behind the table, where once there was a window, are new glass doors leading to the patio—especially convenient when meals are served outdoors.

Storage combines open shelves, glass-doored cupboards, and closed cabinets. The most attractive, most frequently used kitchen equipment appears on the open shelves and glass-faced cabinets; other gear stays in the oak cabinets.

Architect: Thaddeus E. Kusmierski.

Connecting *to kitchen cabinets, dining-height table makes convenient spot for informal meals, becomes buffet counter for patio dining.*

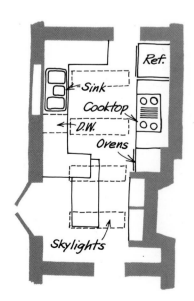

Cooking center *has soffit light; shelf for cook books, spices; hooks for pans.*

Organization with style

Between kitchen chores *owner can step outside to enjoy new deck. Maximum use of glass along wall brings in lots of daylight, offers view of garden.*

With shades down, *kitchen wall looks entirely different. Shades block too-bright sunlight, ensure privacy.*

Cozy breakfast area *makes "L" off kitchen; dining room is through door. Serving as convenient bar is 14-inch-deep cabinet whose bifold doors allow ample clearance between bar and breakfast table. Cook book shelf 6½ feet above floor clears tall heads.*

By adding a mere 3 by 9 feet and moving the kitchen over a bit, the owners of this 12 by 9-foot corridor kitchen gained a breakfast area, a view of the garden, ample light, generous storage and counter areas, and a bar. A new small deck extends from the kitchen.

The former kitchen lacked natural light (an outside structure blocked the small existing windows), counter space, and storage.

Blue cloth-backed vinyl wall covering brightens the new kitchen. Inside the drawers and cabinets is another practical vinyl, this one in a canework pattern. The distinctive blue and white window shades are made of a fabric that was first given a water and stain resistant treatment, then laminated to a backing.

With the help of a skillful and cooperative carpenter (and a plumber, electrician, and other subcontractors called in when necessary), the owners achieved maximum use of space. By such devices as a 3-inch toe space instead of the usual 4-inch one, and routing pipes to try to preserve the original high ceiling, they made valuable extra inches appear.

The white cabinets contain specialized storage drawers: metal bins line a drawer for flour and sugar; wooden dividers organize cutlery drawers; a special deep drawer contains the wastebasket.

There are many practical details. For example, a removable kick panel underneath the dishwasher, held in place by magnets, lets a repairman reach the mechanism. To clear the gas pipe, the top drawer under the cooktop has a notch cut in its back panel.

A mix of gloss and semigloss polyurethane gives the oak floor a medium sheen that looks like a waxed surface. Worn Caucasian rugs have a warmth and traditional look that softens the clean, flat lines of the cabinetry, and the rugs' pattern and color hide food stains.

Designing and Interiors: Barbara Jones Light, ASID.

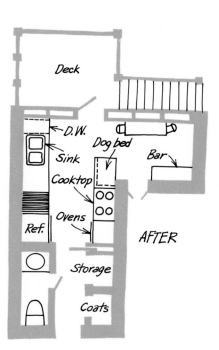

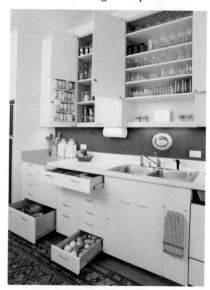

Tightly organized *wall includes butcher-block counter section, drawers for specific purposes–dry vegetables, for example, keep well in drawer with pegboard bottom over ventilating holes drilled through kick panel.*

Beagle-size chamber *built into base cabinet lets dog feel at home. Pad with washable cover fits inside. Drawers above dog bed are extra deep; cabinet has shallow shelves to store cans.*

Meticulously planned *storage includes compartmented drawer (with slide-out shelf below), deep drawers under cooktop for pots and pans and casseroles, and pull-out food rack.*

A happy blend of old & new

Cheerful fireplace *glows at one end of kitchen. Through French doors is attractive garden.*

A comfortable kitchen with all the amenities, modern and otherwise, was the goal here. Contributing to the effect is a wall of used brick that frames a flickering, cozy fireplace—traditional counterpoint to the microwave oven across the kitchen.

Hub of kitchen activity is the tile-topped island. Generous counter space surrounds the burners-plus-barbecue cooktop. Drawers and cupboards on the interior side of the island make it a storage unit.

When they set about remodeling the kitchen, the owner and designer wanted to preserve the character of the older house, yet add more space and more conveniences. An unused porch was integrated into the kitchen. French doors—the new access to the garden—let in much sunlight and offer a pleasant view.

The wide, small-paned windows above the sink admit natural light, too. And all the white surfaces (even the refrigerator, dishwasher, and trash compactor are white-paneled to match the cabinets) help make the room bright and airy.

Designer: John Avram.

Two people can work in this kitchen without feeling crowded. Cooktop vents downward, requires no overhead hood.

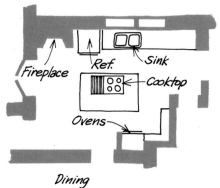

Array of doors conceals pantry, washer and dryer, cookware. Island is conveniently close to both microwave and conventional wall ovens.

New . . . but the old charm remains

Many people who buy older houses to renovate find the kitchens awkward to work in and badly in need of updating. Such was the case with this kitchen, whose owners wanted a modern, efficient room but didn't want to sacrifice any of the charm of their vintage house.

The remodeling process revealed a brick chimney wall which the owners decided to leave exposed. They installed wooden cabinets, created bay windows—one behind the sink and one in the family eating area—and selected patterned tile for the counter backsplash. The background color of the tiles repeats in the tiled countertop. Adding to the country kitchen atmosphere are gingham-patterned wallpaper and the traditional chandelier above the dining table.

The U shape provides plenty of work space—enough to be shared by two or three cooks at the same time. Cooktop and wall ovens are located opposite the sink, and a large pantry cabinet holds food. Over the cooktop, the custom-built ventilating hood contains a copper insert that adds a cheery glow.

Family gathers around *wooden chopping block peninsula that serves as work counter for cutting and chopping tasks. It doubles, too, as snack counter and divider, permitting people to be nearby but not underfoot.*

Bay window *added on behind sink frees enough space for large Boston fern, widens view for person at sink.*

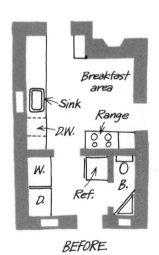

BEFORE

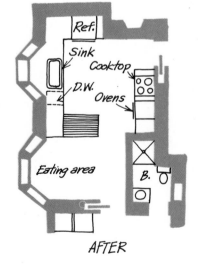

AFTER

Cooking center *contains cooktop, wall ovens. Large, deep drawers below cooktop store casseroles, sizeable pots.*

Open beams make kitchen seem bigger

These curved, open ceiling beams form a repeat pattern of floating forms, breaking up the long and narrow overall space.

The homeowners' goals in remodeling were to expand the eating area that adjoins the kitchen, add telephone and desk space, enclose all storage, and introduce bright color into the room.

Traffic still circulates through this kitchen, but it stays to one side, out of the way of most work functions and the eating area.

A color-filled peninsula divides the kitchen from the breakfast area. Sliding panels open from both sides; inside are electrical outlets. Thanks to the raised part of the peninsula, people sitting in the breakfast area see no kitchen clutter.

Double pantries next to the refrigerator ensure plenty of storage—meeting one of the homeowners' goals.

Yellow walls and ceiling, orange counters, wood cabinets, orange sheet vinyl floor covering, and a blue desk make this kitchen colorful.

Architect: James Jennings.

Geometric curves, angles, and straight edges combine in colorful kitchen's structure. Even space-saving double sink angles around corner.

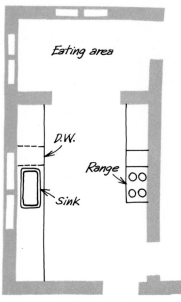

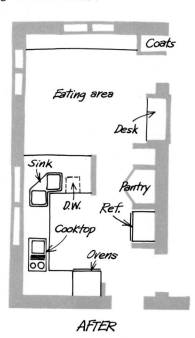

BEFORE

AFTER

Geometry continues to desk at end of kitchen. Triangular opening helps light stairs leading to basement.

Pleasant place to linger, dining room/breakfast area/kitchen flow together to form one large space. Blue and white latticework wallpaper frames view from dining room.

Removing barriers between kitchen and dining room

Making an asset of window with bad view, plants drape down over series of shelves. Stained-glass panel at bottom of window just happened to fit.

Once this kitchen was walled off from the rooms around it and dimly lighted by a lone window over the sink. Taking out a series of doors and cutting through the wall to the dining room made it seem twice as big as it used to be.

In an open eating area that replaced a separate pantry and back porch, new windows bring in daylight. The archway connecting kitchen and dining room joins the two rooms in the style used elsewhere in the house. Blue lattice-pattern wallpaper accents the arch.

White walls in the kitchen and breakfast area reflect maximum light and allow plants to thrive.

The kitchen still utilizes a pantry, but now it's right at hand instead of through a door in another room. The pantry replaces wall cabinets, which could have blocked light.

A combination of counter materials adds practicality: maple flooring tops all counters except the one around the sink, which is a water-resistant, neutral-colored laminated plastic. The sink itself has a high curved bar spout and hospital controls that turn off and on at the push of a forearm—great when hands are soapy.

Architects: Sortun-Cahill-Granger.

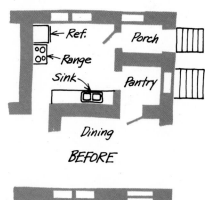

BEFORE

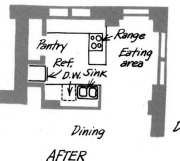

AFTER

Pantry in the middle of U-shaped kitchen replaces overhead cupboards, frees wall space for window. Shelved pantry doors swing out, laden with supplies.

For a new look, try cabinet face-lifts

Leg of U-shaped kitchen extends outward so cooks, kibitzers can gather around it. Where heavy wood beam runs across ceiling, wall once isolated eating area.

New paint on the cabinet structure and two kinds of new cabinet doors give this kitchen a fresh look. Oak doors on the base cabinets contrast handsomely with the blue framework; new stained-glass doors on the wall cabinets add variety and let the cook see the equipment.

When this kitchen was remodeled, a wall between the kitchen and breakfast area was removed—not only had the breakfast area been almost too small to use, but just reaching it had required that the owners open and shut a door. Now a beam supports the ceiling, defining the two rooms without disrupting the space. A bonus is that the beam makes a handy place to hang plants.

The kitchen's practical U-shaped floor plan remained. Wall ovens and cooktop replaced the stove, though, and new cabinet work was constructed around the ovens in the same style as the existing cabinets.

The new oak floor has a Swedish finish, a very durable penetrating resin that must be applied by professional installers.

Storage in this kitchen was kept general, so tools can be rearranged when desired. Generalized storage is also less expensive to build.

The owners used a contractor but saved money by doing their own demolition work.

Architects: Keith Vaughan, Gary Wakatsuki of Joyce, Copeland, Vaughan, and Nordfors. Leaded glass design: Gary Wakatsuki.

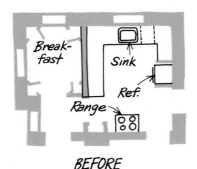

BEFORE

Two kinds of countertops *meet in corner of kitchen. Waterproof laminated plastic is next to sink; butcher block tops other counters. Band of Mexican tile accents splashback.*

Series of shelves *keeps tablewares convenient to eating area.*

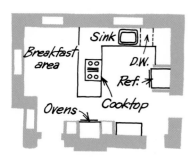

AFTER

New cabinets *support double wall ovens, were built where range once stood.*

Handy shelf *supplements counter; bar behind bowls keeps them from falling.*

The kitchen's behind the pass-through

Table setting *goes fast with pass-through, leaving time for coffee break. In kitchen, wood cabinetry supplements cabinets faced with colored sliding panels.*

Kitchen side *of pass-through has generous expanse of blue laminated plastic countertop; sliding glass doors are neat touch on cabinet above. Wall ovens face refrigerator. Through open door is convenient laundry/sewing/workroom.*

Bold graphics center attention on the pass-through between kitchen and dining room; even the table has a red stripe. The graphics that splash color across this new kitchen and on its pass-through wall echo the forms used elsewhere in the house.

The pass-through adds convenience as well as drama: the cook can slide casseroles and table settings back and forth through the oval cutout in the dividing wall, saving steps.

Inside the kitchen, bright red and blue laminated plastic surfaces are easy to clean, and the bold primary colors raise the spirits. White walls and floor plus a skylight make this compact pullman kitchen very light.

Architect: Wendell Lovett.

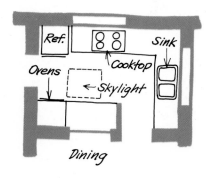

A kitchen planned for plants

Cook's-eye view *shows greenhouse wall section abounding with many kinds of plants. Large surface area of island gives plenty of working space.*

Eating area side of island features storage drawers and cabinets.

Open design plus a tall stretch of thermal glass distribute sunshine to the owner's many plants. The kitchen, dining area, and greenhouse extension form one large room; a sitting room is off to one side.

While working at the generous kitchen island, the cook can talk to her guests or enjoy her plants; there aren't any walls to get in the way. The island boasts concealed storage on both the kitchen side and the dining area side. It surrounds two structural posts which the owner has used to advantage, hanging molds and other decorative utensils on them.

Full-height pantry-type closets store dishes. A microwave oven and warming oven flank the conventional oven.

Architects: The Hastings Group.

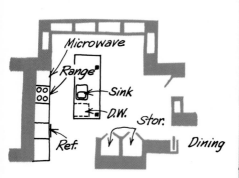

Open shelves hold all manner of cookware. Spice jars line up one deep on lowest shelf; pots and pans hang from row of hooks fastened to underside of another shelf. Blue laminated plastic brightens splashback.

White walls, cabinets, ceiling make kitchen seem larger than it really is, reflect ample light for plants. Counter in corner expands vital work space between sink and cooktop.

Sculptural forms in an all-white kitchen

This kitchen is perfect for a cook who wants everything cleaned up and put away. Streamlined white laminated plastic cabinets and countertops plus built-in appliances contribute to its spick-and-span appearance. Recessed lighting makes the ceiling a flush surface.

This is a one-cook kitchen, with foot traffic diverted away from the busiest work areas. The kitchen opens to a small breakfast area and a deck beyond. On the other side, a round cutout in the wall gives views into the rest of the house.

The owner is a collector but likes to keep her finds put away. Lots of cabinet space lets her store everything but a few selected pottery pieces.

Modern appliances help keep this kitchen immaculate. A micro-wave oven built into the wall above the regular oven cooks without fuss. Because the house sits at the top of a hill, the trash compactor is a special asset—it reduces the number of treks up and down.

Designer: William K. Stout.

Sculptural cabinets *open up extra space for table and chairs. This section of counter, outside main work triangle, is handy for spread-out preparations and serving people at table. Cook can look out to deck through sliding glass doors.*

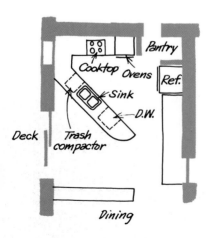

Pantry

Cooktop Ovens

Ref.

Sink

D.W.

Deck

Trash
compactor

Dining

Circular cutout *gives glimpse of rest of house, makes kitchen seem less enclosed and separate. Long counter can double as buffet; storage space inside wall cabinets extends to ceiling.*

A natural kitchen—for country cooking

Angled counters create extra working space. Overhead light fixtures point directly down; small skylight in center of kitchen supplements electric light.

Walking from the vegetable garden into this kitchen built of natural materials is a logical progression. What's more, atmosphere and practicality work hand in hand here: this country kitchen is both efficient and easy to keep up.

Cedar walls set the rustic stage. Since the laminated fir counter is thick—3 inches thick—the owner chops and slices on it without worrying about nicking or scratching it; boat nails trim the counter edging. Adding another element of mellow utility is a wide, one-of-a-kind hammered copper sink. And the sturdy aggregate floor sweeps clean in no time.

Extra-wide counters let the cook spread out ingredients and utensils without running out of space. Open shelves and lots of hooks on the walls keep culinary tools a short reach away.

Setting cooktop burners at an angle left space between and in front of them to put down a coffee cup or balance a mixing bowl. The refrigerator is tucked away in the pantry along with shelf-loads of staples and bunches of dried herbs.

Architect: J. Alexander Riley.

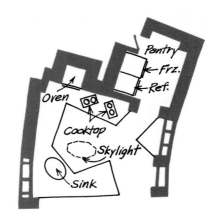

It's an open-and-shut kitchen

When the folding doors are pulled across this kitchen, linear graphics intrigue the eye. And the fresh, bold theme carries through the appliances, shelves, and counters inside the kitchen.

The graphic magic was worked with paint—an inexpensive, easy-to-change way to decorate. Counters of colored plastic laminate are a bit more permanent.

Because it can be closed off behind the doors, this is very much a work kitchen rather than a display kitchen. Tools and ingredients are out on open shelves. After preparing a complicated meal, the cook can simply pull the doors across the kitchen entrance and sit down with guests. Never mind cleaning up—the kitchen literally disappears.

This is a quite small kitchen, but its practical U shape maximizes counter space and helps make it efficient.

Designer: L. Jarmin Roach, ASID.

Open, doors fold neatly out of the way. Walls, other surfaces of kitchen continue graphic design. Accessible open shelves run along kitchen walls.

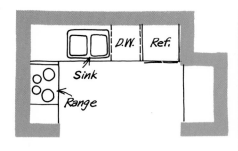

Closed, doors display vibrant linear graphic, adding drama to adjacent room. White floor and ceiling help make small space seem larger.

Glass cabinet doors don't just show off tableware; used on both kitchen and dining area sides, they let light pass through from room to room. At far left, built-in spice cabinets also use glass.

They built a kitchen in the treetops

From inside this small, compact kitchen the cook enjoys sunshine and a marvelous treetop view, and she talks to her guests through large "interior windows" opening to the living room and the dining area. The central location of the kitchen dictated the design of this level of the house.

What's more, this kitchen meets some seemingly irreconcilable requirements of the cook. She likes to see her guests and talk to them, but prefers to do the actual cooking by herself, at the same time sparing others the sight of meal-preparation clutter. She likes to see what's in her cupboards (in closed cabinets a seldom-used casserole or set of bowls can be forgotten) but has reservations about open shelves because the contents get dusty.

The architect's answers were to install glass-doored cabinets and to make openings in some of the walls to create interior windows above counter level. The effect is a kitchen set slightly apart, open to the trees outside.

The owners did finishing work on the kitchen themselves. Many hours spent hunting through antique stores and flea markets led to the discovery of the leaded glass used in the cabinets. Base cabinets are built of redwood plywood; pulls on these cabinets are used porcelain doorknobs selected to match the smaller porcelain pulls above.

Big roll-out drawers and a built-in spice cabinet add convenience. The practical tiled counter contains a recessed wood chopping block next to the sink. A quarry tile floor stands up to heavy use.

Architect: Glenn Pollock.

Windows open wide, bringing fresh air into this open-feeling kitchen. Ledge running just above counter holds miscellaneous jars, condiments. Interior window (right) opens to living room.

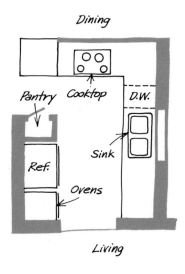

Dining

Pantry Cooktop D.W.

Sink

Ref.

Ovens

Living

Height of overhead cabinets was calculated carefully—they are just above eye level, yet low enough to be reached into easily.

Ceiling cutout opens kitchen to second story

Sunlight filters through ceiling cutout over kitchen sink; windows on two stories let in maximum light. Hanging plants are easy to water from balcony on second level of house.

Looking down *from second story is one way to see angled counter section behind sink. African violets enjoy environment there.*

A two-story window wall lights this versatile kitchen. Light and air circulate through the ceiling opening; plants drape down into the kitchen from the level above.

The ceiling cutout opens communications between the kitchen and the second story. A buzzer system—four bells wired to connect the kitchen with the four upstairs bedrooms—signals when dinner's ready. The family members upstairs reply to the cook through the cutout connecting the two floors.

The long, freestanding island functions differently here than in most kitchens and works in a number of ways. Its length creates a corridor floor plan for working purposes. Opening on the kitchen side of the island are numerous drawers and cabinets of different sizes. Also, the freestanding counter forms a gallery/corridor that diverts foot traffic away from the cooking.

The colorful tile floor, walls, and counters show off against the dark-stained flush doors of the cabinets.

Architects: Churchill-Zlatunich Associates AIA.

Guests and family *gather around end of counter to sample appetizers before sitting down to meal. Adjustable track lights distribute light along length of island.*

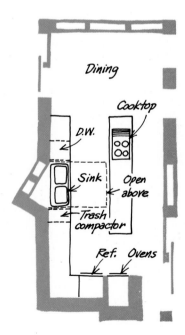

She wanted a pantry
instead of overhead cupboards

In pantry, corner cabinet stores apples, oranges, walnuts, onions. Air circulates through triangular wire shelves. Owner can walk in and, at a glance, see all supplies displayed on floor-to-ceiling open shelves.

Cozy window seat fits in projecting glassed-in alcove off dining room. Low wall, dropped ceiling, hanging plants separate kitchen and dining room.

Kitchen desk has its own wall phone, bulletin board. Window brings daylight for recipe-reading, plants.

Rolling out pastry *is easier on movable marble slab. Big kitchen lets several people work together. Pegboards, knife rack, and mug rack add extra storage.*

The owner of this house started with a few simple requirements for the kitchen: no overhead cabinets, a pantry complete with cooler, and a play area nearby for the children. All were met. No overhead cabinets block the view; the pantry opens off the kitchen; and the children's play area connects to the dining room.

The absence of overhead cupboards and the artfully arranged windows keep the kitchen open and give it an airy feeling. It is big enough for several people to come in and work in different areas. Cascading house plants screen it from the dining area, creating an effective division without blocking light or conversation.

In the kitchen, white walls with redwood trim set off parquet wood counters and a quarry tile floor. A stainless-steel double sink and a range with a built-in grill ease meal preparation.

A low counter between the range and the refrigerator functions as a desk for meal planning and telephoning.

Architect: J. Alexander Riley.

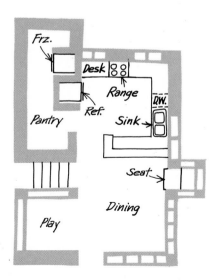

A small kitchen without a closed-in feeling

Windows plus skylight *brighten compact kitchen. High ceiling matches that in living room. At one end of kitchen is sitting room with fireplace; informal eating area is through doorway at other end of kitchen.*

The owners planned this kitchen to eliminate overhanging upper cabinets, make preparation areas as compact as possible, bring in sunlight, and take advantage of the room's orientation.

Instead of using overhead cabinets, they built a series of on-counter storage compartments with tilt-up, slide-back doors. The compartments keep supplies within easy reach, yet conceal them to avoid a cluttered look. In the middle of a cooking project, the cook can put excess ingredients out of the way on the second level. Using the top of the compartments as a cross between a counter and a shelf almost doubles the work space.

Black oak cabinets and unfinished black oak counter edging provide the handsome glow of wood. Leather-look laminated plastic countertops in the U-shaped section of the kitchen give a textured appearance. Tile in a blue and orange pattern lines the cooktop section.

The tiled area is the start-to-finish work zone of the kitchen. Proceeding from refrigerator to auxiliary sink and cooktop to oven, the cook can prepare a complete meal along this one wall. A single portable chopping block is this cook's choice; he often carries it from one part of the kitchen to another. Providing additional work space is the U-shaped part of the kitchen. The leg of the U nearest the ovens is a baking center with a built-in food processor. The other leg of the U is a pivot away from the refrigerator.

Recessed above the tiled area is an expanded version of the traditional plate rail idea. It is wide enough for plants, which enjoy the skylight. The cooktops are electric, far enough away from the plants that heat doesn't bother them.

Designer: R. Paul Bradley.

Orange patterned tile adds extra beauty to utility; hot pans go directly from cooktop to counter. Tiled splashback wipes clean easily. Deep pots and pans fit underneath sink's curved spout. Even this auxiliary sink has garbage disposer to save steps.

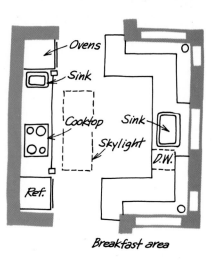

Breakfast area

Counter-level storage compartments extend all around U. Some have built-in electrical outlets, so appliances just pull out onto counter for use.

Usually wasted space, corners display potted plants dropped into circular cutouts. Copper liners contain water overflow, pull out for emptying.

Examples 61

Breakfast preparation *goes fast in kitchen that is small, efficient. Kitchen also works well for frequent dinner parties; dining table is visible through door next to refrigerator.*

Less floor space, more counter space

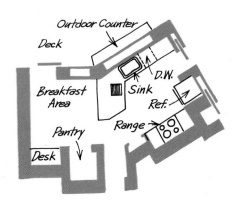

This small kitchen boasts generous counters, and the vivid red tile countertops and orange tile backsplashes make the most of these lavish expanses.

An extra-wide, angled counter divides the kitchen from the pantry/breakfast/office area. Knee space underneath the counter lets the cook sit while using the built-in chopping block.

Both kitchen and eating area capture a sweeping view where the house changes angles. Big windows and sliding glass doors open to a

deck; a counter extension just outside a window acts as a pass-through for serving outdoor meals.

This informal kitchen requires a minimum of maintenance. The patterned resilient flooring (from which tile colors were picked up) and tile counters with natural grout clean quickly and easily.

Architects: Churchill-Zlatunich Associates AIA.

Chopping-block insert lets cook slice away without damaging counter; scraps are whisked into sink. Stool and knee space make tedious chores easier. Deep corner between knee space and sink plumbing holds large coffeepot.

Extra-large drawer stores toaster until it's needed. Electrical cord passes through cutout in back of drawer; toaster stays plugged into outlet.

Window slides open, creating pass-through for meals outdoors on deck. Coffeepot sits on ledge extension outside window.

A kitchen built with Mexican art objects

Pigskin-covered table in center of kitchen is warm, informal place to be. Nearby, tall storage unit wraps partway around brown-toned refrigerator.

A nonstop 10-year love affair with Mexico was the beginning of this kitchen. The owners collected old hardware, Mexican antiques, doors, tiles, and accessories—then asked the designer to pull them together.

Beneath the façade of Mexican artifacts is an efficient kitchen. Double ovens, refrigerator, gas cooktop, and sinks are all there, but they bow to the Mexican motif.

The center chandelier from Oaxaca hangs near a skylight in the beamed ceiling. Miniature clay dishes form a starry pattern on the plaster wall, and the bird cage—Mexican, of course—houses a singing canary.

Designer: Cliff May.

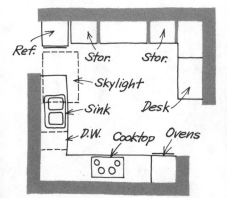

Strands of garlic and dried flowers *accent range area. Arch stores firewood, baskets of potatoes and onions. Saucepans hang above cooktop; terra cotta pots hold wooden Mexican spoons and tools, all used in cooking.*

Ceramic brazier *brings cheer, takes chill off cold and rainy nights. Counter that holds it is used for serving.*

Details: It's the small things that count

1

2

3

4

5

6

The little things count, especially when you're trying to make kitchen chores go faster and easier. For example, neatly dividing pan lids will save time and disposition—you won't have to fumble through a pile of rattling lids for the one you need. Even something as mundane as the placement of the trash can makes a difference in the smooth flow of kitchen work.

In this chapter we illustrate innovative solutions to the smaller problems of kitchen design. Look over the photographs for ideas you can adapt to make your own kitchen more functional. If your kitchen needs help but you don't want to

1) Movable butcher's block *adds to kitchen's counter space. Designer: E. J. Freck.*

2) One-third *of handy kitchen island is actually a marble-topped cart. Architect: Marvin Witt, Jr.*

3, 4) Wooden cart *goes to dining room loaded with dishes and food, returns after meal with dirty dishes. Commercially manufactured cart fits into island designed to store it.*

5) Topped *with wooden cutting board, cart rolls wherever surface is needed for chopping, cutting tasks.*

6) Serving cart *disappears into kitchen island when not in use. Flip-up extensions add to cart's surface area. Architects: A. O. Bumgardner and Partners.*

completely remodel it, an inspiration or two from this chapter may be just what you're looking for.

On pages 68–69, close-up photographs of baking centers show you diverse ways to store flour and sugar, mixing bowls and measuring cups; here, too, are ideas for work surface material and placement. Desks in the kitchen are reviewed on page 70. Study the photographs for ways to fit a desk into your kitchen layout and for methods of storing cook books and other paraphernalia.

Ways to store table linens—place mats, napkins, and tablecloths—are on page 71. Handling a kitchen trash can is the subject of the photographs on page 72. Turn to page 73 to see an array of spice storage ideas.

If a pantry would solve some food storage problems, check the variations of the pantry idea shown on pages 74–75. Storing such small appliances as toasters, mixers, and can openers is the subject of the illustrations on pages 76–77. You'll find systems of organizing cooking utensils—from wire whips to stock pots—on pages 78–79.

At left, serving carts of many types point up the alternatives available. Not only do styles of carts vary, but the ways the carts fit into the total kitchen layout vary also. These examples can help you decide what's best for your particular situation.

A selection of baking centers

Wall and island work together when bread is made here. Grain mill pulls out of cabinet; in drawer below are tin-lined compartments. Kneading machine stays on swing-up stand. (For more views, see page 24.)

Built-in sifters for flour, sugar speed baking. Units slide out for refilling. Architect: George Cody.

Marble insert makes nonstick surface for candy, pastry making. Small appliances plug into strip outlets; baking equipment fills trays, drawers below counter. Designer: John Scaduto, Mayta and Jensen.

Mixer on swing-up stand, special drawers for flour complete baking center conveniently positioned next to oven. Architect: James T. Flynn.

Lowered mixing counter measures 32 inches high; other counters have 36-inch working height. Open shelf holds herbs, spices; stool fits in slot underneath counter. Designer: Janean.

Self-contained center includes appliance storage with strip outlets, spice shelves, metal-lined drawers for flour, sugar. Architect: Otto Poticha.

Desks in the kitchen

Well-equipped planning center has lowered counter section as work surface, includes telephone, shelves.

Menu planning, correspondence take place at desk—an extension of counter. Architects: Joyce, Copeland, Vaughan.

Home office takes up one wall next to eating island. Book shelves and pigeonholes for records and correspondence extend from overhead cabinets. Chalkboard at end of office area, made of sheet of satin-finish plastic laminate that matches countertops, centralizes reminders, lists. Architect: Robert W. Champion.

Ways to store table linens

See-through cabinet's shelves are accessible from dining room or kitchen.
Designer: The Richardson Associates.

Shallow, pull-out shelves store place mats, other table linens flat. Architect: James T. Flynn.

Large wooden dowels attached to metal drawer slides pull out for table-cloth choice. Architect: Loren D. Durr.

Drawers facing dining area keep table linens close at hand. Designer: Janean.

Here's where to put the trash

Commercial plastic container fits into tip-out bin underneath sink.

Round cutting board lifts into place to conceal countertop opening to trash container. Architect: Jacob Robbins.

Door in tiled wall gives access to metal trash chute. Architects: Donald James Clark, Thomas Higley.

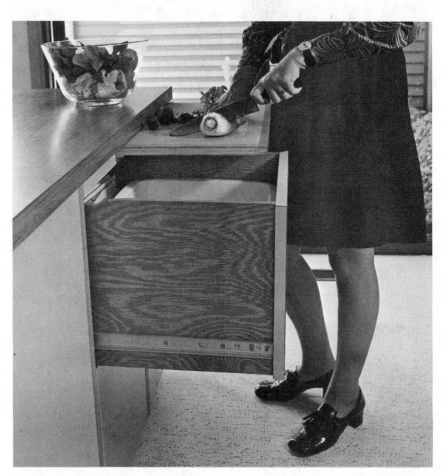

Drawer under cutting board holds plastic trash basket. Architect: Marvin Witt, Jr.

Storing spices

Storage cabinet slides out on metal drawer guides. Center panel separates containers. Designer: E. J. Frech.

Recessed shelves, built between studs, are concealed behind door. Architect: Bruce Starkweather.

Two shallow open shelves store spices next to cooktop. Architect: Hal Gilbert.

Under overhead cabinets, extra shelf has swing-up door. Designer: Leroy Devereux.

Seven variations

Slanted shelves hold canned goods; remove one, the rest roll forward. Architect: Earl Kai Chann.

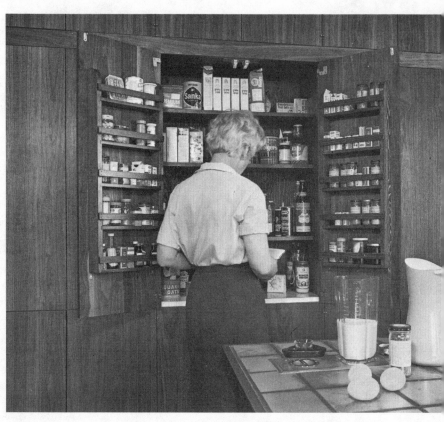

Wall cabinets store canned goods, packaged foods. Racks on doors hold spices, herbs. Architect: Moritz Kundig.

Plastic, perforated, pull-out bins hold potatoes, oranges, other fresh produce. Metal-lined drawers store rice and noodles. Architect: George Cody.

Above washer and dryer, cabinets contain pantry items, extra kitchen utensils. Architect: Charles Metcalf.

of the pantry idea

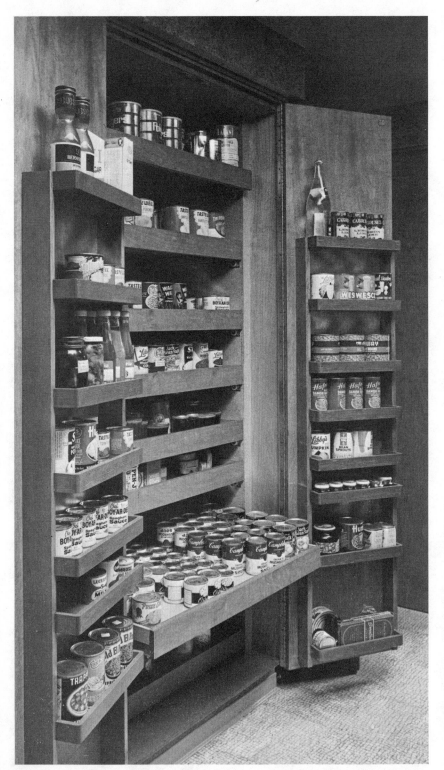

Cut-out shelves in walk-in pantry allow storage one item deep for easy selection. Designer: Charles L. Larson.

Floor-to-ceiling pantry stores food in broad drawers as well as on doors. Drawers pull out to bring contents into view. Architect: Stanley Jacobson.

Perforated hardboard lines pantry door, providing storage for odd-shaped utensils. Architect: A. Jane Duncombe, Duncombe-Roland-Miller.

Small appliance storage

Corner space *above counter in U-shaped kitchen stores condiments, small appliances. Designer: Janean.*

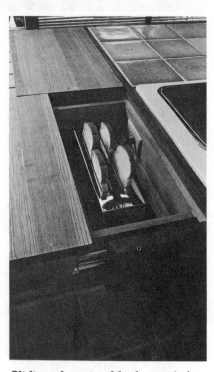

Sliding chopping block *at end of counter hides toaster; silverware, place mats get similar storage treatment. Architect: Paul H. Elliott.*

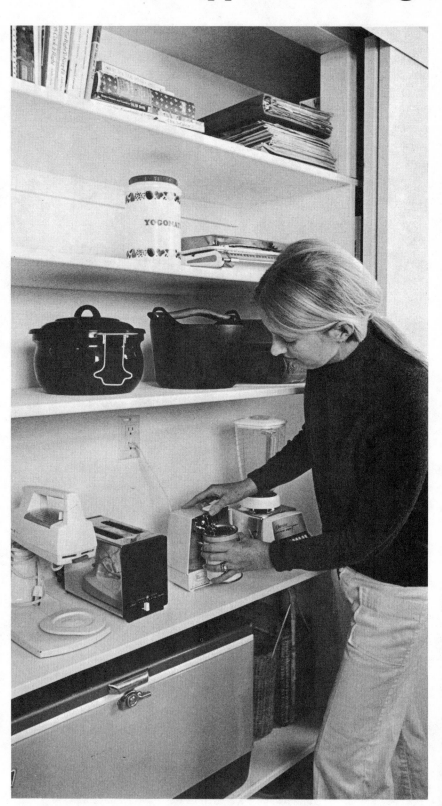

Small appliance shelf *shares large storage area, has electric outlet so appliances are ready to use. Architect: James Flynn.*

76 Details

Power outlet strip runs along rear of cabinet; panels slide to conceal appliances. Architect: Thomas Higley.

Toaster sits in its own niche with electric outlet, on same level as diners seated at parquet eating counter. Architect: Robert W. Champion.

Appliances pull forward on trays outfitted with nylon rollers, hide behind bifold doors when not in use.

Organizing cooking utensils

Perforated hardboard dividers hold platters, serving trays, utensils on hooks. Panels slide out for easy selection. Designers: Mayta and Jensen.

Pans hang from hooks on 1 by 2-inch wood strips nailed to wall studs. Strips are about 8 inches apart, preventing pans from bumping wall surface. Architect: Bruce Starkweather.

Vertical dividers organize baking pans, large serving trays; all items are visible. Architect: Don L. McKee.

Sliding trays loaded with pots and pans pull out from underneath cooktop. Architects: Moyer Associates.

Cooking utensils dangle from wrought iron rack attached to ceiling. Items are easy to reach, decorative. Designer: C. E. Rosebrooks.

Pull-out rack holds cooking pots, pans. Drawer above rack contains dividers to separate pot lids. Architect: James A. Jennings.

Turntable shelves in corner accommodate mixing bowls, muffin tins, molds. Architect: Donald James Clark.

Index

PHOTOGRAPHERS